UNCOVERING INTUITION

UNCOVERING INTUITION

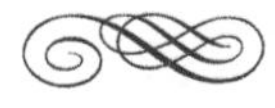

Guidance, Inspiration, and Exercises to Unlock Your Inner Wisdom

SHERYL WAGNER

Sheryl Wagner Medium

First Printing, 2021

For Curtis and Clay—

you are forever an extension of my heart.

ACKNOWLEDGMENTS

To all the remarkable teachers I've had on both sides of the veil, I'm so grateful for your love, guidance, patience, humor, and generosity.

To my partner, Rachel, thank you for finding me, loving me, and building a life with me. I love you endlessly.

To my parents, Curt and Marsha, thank you for your support and encouragement without which none of this would be possible.

Thank you to my younger siblings Rachel and Jayne, my first coven. I love and cherish you both.

To Darren Brittain, thank you for seeing me before I could fully see myself, for helping me turn on the lights, and for being brave enough to stay with me and look around the room. I am forever grateful for your love and support.

To my dear friend Erica Lee, thank you for being my sister, confidant, and inspirer. The best is yet to come.

To Mike, for having the strength and love to grow together and grow apart.

To Taji, thank you for your unwavering belief in me and my story. You inspired me to stand in my truth by bravely standing in yours.

To Josh, for saving my life, keeping my secrets, and urging me along when things seemed unbearable, and to June for encouraging me to tell this story. I love you.

To Katie Malloy Ramaci and Women of Wisdom, thank you for believing in me early on and for the magical place you've created in this world where I feel honored to learn and teach.

To Liam Galvin, for that first reading that changed my life and all the lessons that followed. I love you.

To Rita Berkowitz, thank you for believing in me and for helping me to see clearly.

To Eamon Downey, thank you for sharing your wisdom, kindness, and teachings with me, I am so grateful.

To my grandparents, Don and Marilyn Rodman, thank you for your unwavering faith in me on both sides of the veil. Thank you for always holding me, guiding me, and making space for me, for the years when your love was a home to me. I hope I make you proud.

Thank you to my students, so many of whom have touched my heart and changed me forever. I am honored to be a part of your journey.

Thank you to my clients both here and in the Spirit World, I'm honored to have your trust, to work with and alongside you.

CONTENTS

AUTHOR'S NOTE—HOW TO USE THIS BOOK

There is a version of you beneath ego and personality, beneath the roles you play in your life, i.e. parent, partner, friend. Feel beneath the conditioning and strategies that have helped you survive. Beyond survival, image and identity lies your true nature and a source of power and inner wisdom. You are here for a purpose and discovering that purpose is your divine right. To discover it, you need to go within yourself.

There have and will be many more signs along the way of your inner journey. Roadblocks, detours, and distractions will require your courage, patience, and determination. There will also be signs that grab your attention, ignite your inner fire, make you uncomfortable, and inspire you to seek truth. My hope is that this book is one of *those* signs.

I have spent a great deal of time thinking about who would read this book and what you would need to hear. My story comes to you not at random but through the manifestation of your dreams and mine. We are all connected in our inner journeys towards truth and love.

Use this book as a guide for connecting to and understanding your intuition. The exercises are meant to support, awaken, or expand your spirit and perhaps make you feel less alone. I hope that you will take what feels relevant to you and leave the rest. Scribble notes in the margins if you'd like, practice the meditations in any order that feels right to you, and read the lessons in order of what you feel most curious about.

I hope you will treat yourself with love and compassion as you work to develop and understand your inner wisdom. Please be gentle with yourself as you explore this inner world. Even if we haven't met, I know that you have experienced many kinds of heartbreak and that your soul seeks healing and understanding that you can give to yourself. There is so much magic and mystery ahead for you. You are meant to have a free, spacious, fulfilling life. There are many beautiful moments waiting for you beyond this one. These universal truths connect us.

Love,

Sheryl

P.S. If you would like to share your thoughts, ideas, or how you came to hold this book in your hands I would love to hear from you. To share directly with me email contact@sherylwagnermedium.com.

Introduction

Uncovering My Intuitive Life

When I look at my life and the ways my intuition has helped to shape it, it's easy to be drawn to the dramatic moments when intuition seemed to intervene and save me: The moment I decided not to get in that car or walk out of that house, or the chance meeting that altered my life. I've often felt saved at the last second, course-corrected, diverted.

The truth is when we choose to listen to the subtle energetic guidance—our intuition—which lives naturally within each of us and is always present, we can tap into the magic that lies in the quiet space of every moment. We are not limited in our course corrections. There is no way for us to miss our destiny—we cannot "choose wrong" and go completely off course.

What happens is that we choose wrong, and we feel it. We make concessions that disturb our inner peace and create unrest, and we feel it. When we try to numb, escape, or dismiss this pain, we gaslight ourselves and become disconnected from our intuition. We become comfortable with the unrest. We become so accustomed to pain and disconnection that we forget what alignment feels like.

For me, this disconnection stemmed from tragedy and led to burnout that forced me to realign my life. Now, living in alignment with my intuition and purpose feels so freeing. But it was not always this way.

A Different Sort of Child

When I tell people I am a psychic medium, they typically want to know about my childhood or ask questions about my past, especially:

How did I know I could do this? I don't feel that my life has been any more or less remarkable than anyone else's, with perhaps the exception that it has been uniquely touched by death.

Death has been a theme throughout my life: People close to me have passed and I've had communication with them afterward. I've had dreams that predicted death. My own near-death experience in 2004 answered questions I had always had about the Spirit World and made my purpose clear to me.

Like many people I work with who experienced trauma, I have extremely vivid memories of my childhood and then there are gaps. I can remember standing up, holding onto the bars of my crib, and looking at the shadows on the blank white wall of my bedroom in our apartment. I'm told that I wasn't shy yet; I was quite talkative. My mom tried to convince my preschool teacher that I was a genius because of my extensive vocabulary for my age, but I quickly proved that theory wrong. Once I was enrolled, I would not speak or participate in any of the expected ways. Throughout most of my schooling, I was constantly disappointed as I remained lost in my own mind most of the time, always running late, distracted, and constantly forgetting things.

It was in this apartment where one day I dragged my mother over to meet Josh, the toddler next door. My most significant relationships have all begun this way. I am drawn across the country, across the world, a parking lot, a church aisle, moving through the world instinctively often in opposition to my personality to meet the people I'm meant to meet and have the experiences that I'm meant to have. Meeting Josh was no exception. This first meeting lead to our mothers becoming lifelong friends and with that, we all became a family. Eventually, Josh would become an unlikely but important teacher to me both here and in the Spirit World. The many seemingly random meetings of my life remind me that when we are acting in alignment with our intuition, we don't need to force anything, and we cannot miss what is meant for us.

I didn't speak much in my childhood or adolescence, and it was typical for me to go entire school days in complete silence. I would refuse to answer questions and try to get away with just shaking my head yes or no. But I didn't think my silence was strange except when someone—like my peers or frustrated teachers—would ask, "Why don't you talk?" I remember in high school walking behind a group of girls who I thought I was quite friendly with, listening as one of them struggled to describe who her class partner was. "You know, she's that girl who sneezes a lot, the one that never talks."

Oh right, I thought, that is definitely me.

My silence as a child makes sense to me now, since as an adult I was diagnosed with inattentive ADHD. But I also think of myself as a highly sensitive person who struggles to cope with overstimulating environments.

I didn't realize it at the time, but there was a lot happening for me in my silence. What had begun as a coping strategy gave me the space and freedom to develop a rich inner world that would eventually cultivate my connection to the Spirit World and to my own inner knowing. Although various traumas have caused me to struggle to stay connected to my body and intuition—and at times I have put parts of myself away in order to conform to expectations and achieve things throughout my life—my intuition has been the thread that's silently pulled me along, saving me, and eventually leading me to create a life I love.

The ADHD diagnosis came in my thirties. If I would have received this diagnosis sooner it may have mitigated many of my early struggles, especially as I tried to regulate my inattention with substances throughout my adolescence. If I had understood my neurodivergence, I could have treated it with medication and been better able to deal with my environment.

Instead, I used everything I could just trying to fit in, manage my anxiety around feeling different or to just disappear. As a kid, it meant not speaking and then developing an eating disorder, which allowed me to become smaller and feel invisible. As a young teenager, I turned to pills and alcohol to self-regulate.

After I confessed to smoking marijuana at a temple youth group, my parents decided I should attend Narcotics Anonymous meetings where I met an array of interesting characters. The meetings were not helpful to me as a struggling teenager, but I liked them because everyone said exactly what they were thinking, which was comforting.

Intuitive people recognize both truth and the lack of it, and an authentic truth connection was missing from my life. I recognize now that as a highly sensitive person when someone is lying or being ingenuine it takes a lot of energy for me to feel comfortable in their presence.

Beyond substance abuse and restrictive eating, I tried to disappear by disconnecting from my body. I spent most of my time thinking and imagining, which allowed me to escape feeling my emotions. But the truth is, this disconnection began during a moment that is much more difficult to talk about.

When I was fourteen years old, I was sexually assaulted by a man who was supposed to be driving me home. I know the exact moment my body entered complete disconnection and survival mode: Looking out the car window, I saw only a dark dirt road on either side; I weighed about ninety pounds and was miles away from anything that could help me.

To survive that trauma, I had to completely disconnect from my body and my mind. Experiencing this at the beginning of adolescence meant I would continue to hide parts of myself away for years. Especially when it came to being gay.

Whenever I felt threatened after that assault, I disconnected from my body. Because I couldn't be fully present, I didn't develop a healthy expectation of feeling safe in romantic relationships and eventually ended up in an abusive relationship in my late teens. But after escaping that relationship, I met my ex-husband, Mike in one of those random meetings that seem to happen to me. Mike was kind and in contrast to my prior relationships, I felt safe with him. I am grateful for our relationship, not only because we have two children together, but because our relationship—and ultimately our friendship—allowed us both a safe space to grow.

I realize now that being married to a man kept me somewhat safe emotionally. Though I knew I was attracted to women, I didn't come out publicly until my children were teenagers. The more I tapped into my intuition and learned how to use my psychic/mediumistic abilities, the more I felt comfortable in my body. Eventually, coming out as gay was the natural next step in becoming me.

Breaking Down and Breaking Through

Inattentive ADHD causes me to get lost in my own thoughts and remain quiet instead of running around making lots of noise like the Hyperactive Attention Deficit Disorder we tend to associate with kids. For me, the noise and chaos are internal and often not visible to others.

One night when my own kids were babies, I was working a waitressing job I loved. It was a busy night at the restaurant and as I raced around, I was blindsided by an important guest who was a local celebrity—my boss watched in horror as I almost ran her over. Then I served bread with pine nuts in it to a table with a nut allergy. The guests at the table promptly asked to speak with the manager, who had just finished consoling the guest I had almost knocked over. I remember my boss saying to me, "You're smart, you care, I feel like you could do anything. I can't put my finger on what's wrong with you, but you've got to get your shit together or you can't work here."

I was in total agreement with him and couldn't put my finger on it either, so I quit. I believed that there was something wrong with me that had yet to be discovered and I wasn't quite ready to face what.

After that job, when I started to make sense of my neurological differences and treat myself accordingly, things started to improve. I went back to work for my family business selling cars, which I loved. I was successful there because I was very good at reading people and knowing what they would want when a customer would walk into the showroom, or when someone was wasting time and I needed to let them go.

In the middle of one of our busiest sales weekends of the year, our finance manager walked out. Because my boss was desperate and with a showroom full of customers waiting to sign for the vehicles they had just purchased, he asked me to fill in as finance manager.

It took an excruciating six months for me to become not only proficient at the paperwork, but I soon developed a better sense of myself and stronger boundaries. I was elated—finally I was great at something! My ability to read people or know which pressure points to work with the banks helped get my deals done. I like to think that I used my psychic abilities for good, and people responded to my authenticity in truly wanting to help them.

Thriving in this environment meant mostly putting away the sensitive and intuitive parts of myself. In return, I enjoyed financial success and the approval of my family. Before I worked at the dealership, there was a firm policy that no women from the family were allowed to work in the business.

But my grandfather made an exception for me because he felt I was a hard worker. I'm sure he thought my extremely unemotional and quiet ways were a benefit, which was probably also why I was one of the highest-paid employees in the company. As a thirty-something woman working in the auto industry I had to fight extremely hard to justify my salary, which was defined by my monthly revenue goals and could be tracked to the penny on an Excel spreadsheet. As my dad (who was also my boss) loved to point out, "You make more than your husband, for crying out loud."

If you'd asked me, I'm sure I would have said I was healthy and happy, but I was still restricting food in a misguided attempt to stay disconnected from my body. At that time, I did not enjoy eating at all and never felt hungry. But my body showed me I needed food when, in the middle of racing around at work, I would suddenly panic because I couldn't feel my feet. So, I would eat a bag of almonds, but they tasted horrible. I was so used to this way of existing that it seemed normal and took years for me to regain feelings of hunger. Even now, sometimes when I am stressed, I crave that lightheaded feeling of starvation.

I've learned that disordered eating looks and feels different for everyone. For me, it was a symptom of my refusal to live as my true self. Being completely disconnected from my body and my emotions meant I couldn't feel much of anything. Knowing myself as I do now—as a deeply emotional and intuitive person who is fulfilled by working with grieving clients—I recognize how much energy it took for me to suppress who I was and work in the cold and aggressive environment of car sales.

But I was definitely tough enough. I rarely showed any emotion at work and would rather have been hit by a car in the showroom than shed a tear, proving to everyone that women were not tough enough to work in this business. I was so completely shut off emotionally that there was a running joke in my family: I didn't even cry when our dog died.

My conditioning had led me to believe that success was defined by making money, taking up the least amount of physical space possible, and not feeling any emotion whatsoever. So the day after my dad had a heart attack, I broke the news to the rest of my management team by sitting in his seat at the head of the conference room table, coolly letting them know that he was probably going to be okay but that we had work to do. I felt really in control of my success...until I wasn't.

In April 2017 after we returned from a family vacation, my son had a severe mental health crisis and required hospitalization. Fearing for his life triggered flashbacks from my own near-death experience, and I ultimately had a breakdown that led me to reconnect to not only my emotions, but my mediumship and intuitive abilities. When I was forced to face the reality that my mental and physical health were in crisis, I could also no longer keep my emotions and awareness of the Spirit World separate.

I began hearing the voices and seeing the loved ones who'd passed of some of my finance clients. Although I had come to understand by then that I was communicating with my own loved ones who had passed to the Spirit World and others that felt familiar to me, I had never heard of mediumship beyond what you'd see on TV in the 90s, or stories of my great grandmother reading tea leaves.

Increasingly, I had this overwhelming feeling that my life was somehow coming to an end, I just couldn't understand how. I'm not sure how to explain this other than to say that I had a knowing that I would die or cease to exist somehow. What I didn't realize was that it was actually true in a sense—my life as I had known it was ending and a new way of being would begin. I made the decision to start sharing this information and my connections to the dead with my therapist.

I was sure she would say that the visions I was experiencing and voices I was hearing meant that I needed hospitalization. But to my surprise, she suggested that I make an appointment to see a medium. She had lost her dad when she was twelve and swore that this Medium had helped her to know her dad was at peace. I emailed to make an appointment but wouldn't learn until three months later—after we had become friends—that this medium was the son of the doctor who had helped me make sense of my medical trauma thirteen years earlier. During the session, he told me I was also a medium, that I was going to start to develop my mediumship, and that I would eventually teach mediumship to others and write a book about my life.

A few months later, I quit my job at the dealership and began doing free mediumship readings out of a small, rented office space. I attended the Arthur Findlay College in the United Kingdom to study mediumship, which ended up being a great confirmation of what I'd been experiencing.

Everything on that trip felt like it was perfectly designed and orchestrated by the Spirit World to support me on my journey. I felt an overwhelming sense of homecoming to myself and returned to Boston with more confidence in my abilities and understanding of who I was and what I must do. I met a woman from Switzerland at the college who had talked about being in a women's empowerment group and now I knew that was something I wanted to create—a place where I could support others in making authentic connections with one another.

When I started a women's empowerment circle in my town, it quickly grew into what is now my weekly mediumship practice circle. After a year, I moved the circle to a spiritual center because I wanted to create a more diverse group. As I conducted private readings and demonstrations and coached developing mediums, my business continued to grow. I traveled back to England and Holland to study mediumship, met some amazing people, and had incredible experiences learning about and working with the Spirit World.

Emotionally, things have developed for me at such a rapid pace, it seems my life has been a perpetual process of coming out over the last three years—first as a medium and then as gay to my children and my community. Sometimes I joke whether the next realization will be that I'm actually an alien living on this planet. Of course, looking back on it all now, I've always known on deeper levels that I was a medium, just as I've always known I was gay. I just didn't have a word for it.

It's never big dramatic moments that create our life, but instead the quiet spaces where we allow ourselves a voice. We have the power to choose which voices to shut down and which to allow space to grow and thrive. Once I began to listen to this inner knowing, everything began to shift. As I wrote down my intentions, they became my life, and my life changed.

It is an ongoing process to stay in alignment with my intuition. The more I do, the more my life opens up in ways beyond my imagination. In this book I'll share how reconnecting to my intuition has transformed my life, and the accidental and intentional ways I've worked to develop an intuitive life.

As I write this, I'm years into my business as a professional medium. I have recovered from my disordered eating. Starving myself was a way to gain control of my life, but once I started making decisions from my intuition, I no longer needed it.

My hope is that by sharing some of my story with you it will help you connect to the magic that is already present within you.

This book can be used as a guide for intuitive development or as a tool as you continue to delve deeper into your own inner wisdom. My greatest wish is to leave you feeling empowered, validated, and more connected to yourself so that you remain (or assume) the role of the ultimate authority in your life. I wish for you to feel as free and vital and loved as you truly are, to feel your own aliveness and purpose stirring within you until it simmers over.

I

Part One

Uncovering Your Intuition—Getting Started

I

An Intuition Primer

Is it Intuition or is it Anxiety?

If you're here, chances are you're curious about exploring your intuition. Perhaps you've had some signals from your life that tell you it's time to tap into your inner voice. Discomfort, fear, and burnout can be powerful clues that we need to turn inward to discover the truth. But we don't need to wait until a crisis moment to listen.

If this is the first time you are considering listening to your intuition, the idea can be frightening. The notion that you know exactly what you want and how to get there can be overwhelming. It can be much more comfortable to throw your arms up and say things are beyond your control and there is nothing you can do. I'm here to tell you that there is so much goodness waiting for you beyond this comfort zone.

Intuition is accessible to everyone as a natural instinct. If we are honest with ourselves, we can admit that there were many intuitive signals leading up to that moment of crisis, but we ignored our inner knowing.

I don't believe in randomness. My life has led me to believe each of our interactions is inexplicably linked to the next until we arrive in our present moment.

Right now, you and I are inexplicably linked, just like everyone and everything that exists. Consider that you are exactly where you are meant to be at this moment, reading these words. Consider how much it took for you to get here, for me to get here. Consider that you have within you the knowledge to create a life that feels better to you—all you need to do is listen to yourself. I realize that sounds far too simple, so let's break this down.

What is intuition? And why do we confuse it with fear and anxiety?

Many highly intuitive people experience frequent anxiety. But with practice and self-awareness, they can begin to rely on and trust their intuition.

Understanding Intuition

Intuition is an instinct, a natural ability to know or understand something without conscious reasoning—it's subtle energetic guidance. Scientists believe intuition operates through the parts of our brain that are responsible for managing creativity, memory, and recognizing patterns. Because our brains are neuronally connected to our digestive system (our gut), many people will experience a "gut feeling" when experiencing intuition.

Though many people think of intuition as a feeling, you may not experience "a feeling" at all. Very often, intuition can feel almost detached, like a wise part of you is operating on your behalf. Intuition feels calm and grounded and is experienced as "a knowing."

Without a doubt, we all have this ability, but everyone has varying levels of sensitivity and awareness. Some people are more naturally gifted because they are highly sensitive or extremely empathic and intuitive; some of us are less so. But we all have intuitive, empathic gifts that can be developed.

When you experience intuition, there is often no need for anxiety because you have "a knowing" of what to do.

Understanding Anxiety

When you experience anxiety, it can be difficult to know whether that's your intuition guiding you, or you are feeling anxious. Intuition is always experienced in the present moment, whereas anxiety based on past experiences and emotions may focus on a future disaster—one that may never happen.

Anxiety is connected to fear, a powerful instinct. It can feel overwhelming and chaotic. Getting to know your unique physical symptoms when you are anxious can help you differentiate between anxious feelings and intuitive guidance.

Moving out of an anxious state helps you "tune into" intuition. I'm not saying to discount fear—it is a lifesaving instinct. However, as humans, we feel fear much more than just a lifesaving amount:

"What if I fail?"

"What if something bad happens?"

"What if I never meet anyone?"

"What will they think?"

If you examine your feelings, you can often identify the why and how of your fear. In reflection or therapy, you can often take your fears back to the root cause. You may discover you are not operating as a conscious being in this moment but are instead operating through all your past experiences.

Your thoughts, behaviors, and feelings link to create your way of being—your conditioning. But this conditioning is one of the largest barriers to trusting and understanding intuition. It doesn't matter if you've had a wonderful childhood or a traumatic one, we have all been raised in and live in a society that regularly dismisses feelings and instincts, but honors productivity over all else. As you start to understand and rely on intuition, it's easier to look back on and understand your conditioning.

Most of us are asked in early childhood to suppress our sensitivity to the world and outright ignore our intuition without complaining. Each time we ask our children to eat more even though they aren't hungry or be polite and hug a relative they don't want to hug; we are asking them to ignore their intuition. We don't need to have had a tough disciplinarian as our caretaker—many of us have been policing and micromanaging ourselves into compliance with familial and societal rules our whole lives. We are, in fact, our harshest disciplinarian or inner critic.

Highly Intuitive people are often more sensitive to this conditioning—we don't even need to hear the words to know how our actions are being perceived. When we walk into a room, we know if an argument has occurred, if someone is uncomfortable around us, or if our pets are in pain. Sometimes we shut down this sensitivity to the world over time, and sometimes we are overwhelmed by it.

More often than not, when a client wants to understand and develop their intuition by working with me, I find that they are highly intuitive, but they have shut down all sensitivity at some point in their life, usually as a coping mechanism. So we begin by examining their conditioning to see how and where it lives in those quiet spaces of their life, blocking their intuition. Though I use the word "block" because it is commonly used in this work, there really is no true block; there's only conditioning masquerading as the only valid choice. Even when my client clearly knows what they want, their conditioning says, "That's ridiculous, what will people think?"

When you explain your position from a place of knowing—when your intuition is guiding you—you sound rational, clear, and grounded. You may not have all the answers, but you know what you want or what needs to be done or not done. When you begin to recognize how intuition speaks to you and how it feels in your body, you feel more confident with decision-making.

Part of knowing how intuition works is knowing how anxiety feels.

When you are experiencing intuition, you may:

- have a strong feeling or knowing
- feel calm and sure of yourself
- know exactly what you truly want or need to do

Where you are experiencing anxiety, you may:

- feel self-conscious
- have tightness in your chest or a quicker heartbeat
- feel restless
- have shortness of breath
- ruminate on thoughts and worries
- have difficulty expressing your feelings and may sound frantic when you try

To determine whether what you're feeling is intuition or anxiety, ask:

- Where do I feel this in my body?
- Is this feeling coming from a calm and grounded place?
- How could my past emotions be influencing me?

Getting Started

Before exploring your intuition, you should know: *Everything is energy.*

As a psychic medium, my job is to communicate with those who have passed to the Spirit World. I see, feel, know, and sense energy, then my mind interprets that energy.

Spirit communication differs from psychic sense or intuition in that we are communicating with a Spirit Person who is very much alive in the other world. But when I talk about energy in intuition, I am speaking about energy on the earth plane.

I realize that not everyone will experience energy to the degree that I see and feel it. In our work together, I need you to know and *believe* the energy of our thoughts, feelings, and emotions is there as well, so we can work with and understand it.

Some things can't be defined by me or you, and it doesn't matter.

Many times, people will ask, "Is this inner knowing connected to my soul? Is it my spirit guides or my grandmother who passed that is guiding me? A guardian angel?"

While it's easy for me to have a general sense of this guiding energy in my own life (or to tune into a client and receive this type of information), I don't know exactly what it is for you—and it truly doesn't matter.

Here's why: If we can accept that everything is energy, that we are all inexplicably linked, and that our mind will conform information to our understanding, then we can begin to let go of defining the specific source of information. We begin to understand there is only one true source: love/truth/Spirit/God/the Universe, or whatever higher power or unseen magic you believe in. But before we can quantify and label the source of our inner knowing or magic, we need to start trusting and believing in it, and in ourselves.

This leads some people to ask the question, "Is that even safe?"

Most of us are conditioned to believe that we should listen to outside voices before listening to our own inner voice. Organized religions or family and community dynamics that lack good boundaries often tell us that we should look outward for approval and answers. While many religions throughout history refer to contacting the Spirit World, the idea that we shouldn't do this ourselves is a common and harmful misconception. Many organized religions thrive on the imbalanced power dynamics that lead us to believe we are somehow disconnected from our intuition and the Spirit World. Even well-meaning spiritual teachers who offer prayers of protection before practicing psychic or mediumship development reinforce the disempowering and harmful idea that we need protection from ourselves or the unseen world.

This is simply not true.

Spirituality itself often feels like organized religion, so it's important for our self-development to not give away our personal power. You are and will remain the ultimate authority in your life, and you do not need anyone's permission to develop and explore your own natural intuitive abilities.

Looking to others for help and guidance is a powerful tool of connection but looking to teachers and gurus for permission and validation can be damaging and disconnecting. Discovering your soul's purpose, living an authentic life, and cultivating your own inner voice cannot be outsourced to someone else.

Which leads me to the next truth: I believe that we are all love at our core. I don't believe in hell or the devil. Throughout this book, the intentions I share will align with the belief that we are love, we come from love, and that the Spirit World is unconditionally loving.

This may be a difficult concept for people to grasp if they have been raised in a religious background and with the punitive nature of a certain god. I was raised Jewish, so it may be easier for me to reject the idea of a punitive god because we do not believe in hell.

As a medium, I have never encountered anything in the Spirit World that was unkind or unloving. I'm not saying I haven't been startled or found one Spirit Person more pleasant or unpleasant than another. I am saying that I have always been safe and encountered love. But since it's something we must experience for ourselves to understand, I don't spend much time trying to convince people of this beyond sharing my own experience.

When I first began practicing mediumship, a close friend called me to share a prayer for protection I should use before "contacting the dead." She had told her friend, a monk, about my work and he convinced her to call me to share this prayer, to ensure that I was not communicating with the devil or other "evil spirits." I have always found this concept odd, although I recognize that many well-meaning and loving people believe it.

I wish only freedom and autonomy of spiritual practice to everyone, and likewise do not need any religion to bless and approve of my life or my spiritual work. I know the Spirit World is all-loving and find that many people easily accept this truth through their own experience.

If you have been raised in a religion that prohibits and does not recognize psychic or intuitive abilities, the process of undoing this conditioning may take time. By going inwards and connecting with your intuition you can develop a set of beliefs that truly resonates with you.

In my work with clients, I find that sharing my personal experiences is often the most direct way to help them connect to their own experience, and to begin putting in place the intuitive development strategies that are right for them.

Throughout this book I will share some stories of how intuition has shown up in my life, the ways I've been disconnected from it, and how I've been able to make my way back to myself. I'll explain the strategies I use to intentionally develop my intuition and in my work with clients. By sharing my own stories and those of various clients (names changed to respect their privacy), I invite you to connect to yourself.

Definition of Terms

The spiritual community has a wide range of terms that aren't understood by many people. When you don't understand a term, refer to this list for understanding and clarity:

Alignment: Alignment refers to a feeling or state when we are living according to our truth and intuition; when we act from our soul or our higher self.

Altar: A dedicated space for spiritual practices. This doesn't need to be anything fancy— it can simply be a table in your room or in a quiet corner of your home. You can use any objects that feel important and connect you to your spiritual practice: written intentions, crystals, photographs of your ancestors, a feather you found on the beach, or whatever is meaningful to you.

Aura: A unique energetic field that surrounds every living thing. Auras can be seen, sensed, and felt, as well as expand and contract. Your aura holds experiences past, present, and future.

Clairaudience: "clear hearing" refers to the ability to perceive energy through hearing sounds, voices, or music. Clairaudience may be subtle—sometimes it feels like you are hearing your own thoughts, or maybe your own voice. Objective clairaudience hearing voices, music, thoughts outside of the mind is also possible.

Claircognizance: "clear knowing" refers to the ability to receive information by knowing. This is the only sense that does not give us the chance to interpret or question, we "just know."

Clairsentience: "clear feeling" refers to the ability of a person to receive information by feeling and sensing energy. All humans have this sense and may develop it.

Clairvoyance: "clear seeing," in mediumship or intuitive work refers to seeing or perceiving information through images or visions. Clairvoyant images may appear in the same space as your imagination but will be clearer and easily recalled. There is also a rarer type of clairvoyance called objective clairvoyance where mediums may see objectively—outside their mind—with their physical eyes.

Conditioning: Our thoughts, behaviors, experiences, and feelings link to create our way of being which I will call "our conditioning" in this book. Our conditioning is one of the largest barriers to trusting and understanding intuition.

Empath, Highly Sensitive Person (HSP), or Highly Intuitive Person (HIP): I tend to use these interchangeably as they have the same general meaning—someone who has a heightened sensitivity to the world around them, including the unseen energetic world. Many of my clients identify as empaths and highly sensitive people who are easily affected by their surroundings including sound, smells, touch.

Intention: Our intent or desired result. Setting intentions before spiritual work or anything of consequence is important. Especially for intuitive people, your intention is the most powerful thing you have in creating your reality.

Intuition: An instinctive ability to understand something immediately without the need for conscious reasoning. Intuition is grounded, clear, calm, and presents as a subtle knowing. All humans and animals have this ability.

Medium: A medium is someone who acts as a bridge between the Spirit World and the earthly world. I work as an evidential medium, meaning I deliver messages and evidence to clients from their loved ones who have passed to the Spirit World.

Precognition: The ability to receive knowledge of a future event or situation, often through extra-sensory perception or psychic sense. Also referred to as premonition, this may be experienced by psychics, mediums, empaths, or highly sensitive people through their heightened senses and awareness. Precognitions may sometimes come to us in the form of a dream, vision, feeling, or knowing. With precognitive dreams or premonition dreams you will remember it vividly, may wake shortly afterward, and the dream will be accompanied by a feeling or knowing.

Psychic: Psychic energy is that of this world. In a psychic reading, I will connect to my client's energy to help gain clarity and guidance around their situation. I will often use "psychic" interchangeably with highly intuitive person. I also tend to use intuition, psychic sense, awareness, or psychic awareness interchangeably. In mediumship there is a common phrase: "All mediums are psychic, however not all psychics are mediums," and this is true in a sense. Everyone who is sensitive enough to connect to the Spirit World will also be able to connect psychically to others in this world.

Psychometry: The act of or ability to perceive information from a place or object. I often use photographs when teaching psychometry.

Soul: Many people use spirit and soul interchangeably, and they are similar. To me, our soul feels more of the human part of us—connected to our higher self, having purpose, strength, and meaning. I believe our souls are on a journey of evolution throughout lifetimes, desiring knowledge, wisdom, and experience to grow and change. I also believe our soul has all the knowledge of everything we've ever known and everything we will ever know, which means they are linked to our intuition. Your soul will undeniably recognize truth and love and be drawn to certain places and people for its evolution.

Spirit: I often use this to describe "the source of everything"—Spirit, God, the Universe, whatever your higher power is. I also use "spirit" to describe your individual spirit— the eternal part of you, your essence, that will return to the Spirit World after your life on Earth.

Spirit guides: Those souls in the Spirit World who are there throughout our lives to guide and inspire us to live in our purpose. Everyone has spirit guides, and everyone's perception and experience of them varies. I encourage you not to be preoccupied with identifying or collecting evidence on specific spirit guides, but rather to just trust what you feel and come to know over time.

Spirit World: The Spirit World or Spirit Realm refers to the unseen world or "place" where our spirit returns after our life on Earth. My experience of the Spirit World is that it is not a far-off place or heaven, but that is all around us, all the time, exists beyond time and space, and—while we are human—operates on infinite love and intelligence beyond our comprehension. My knowledge of the Spirit World comes from my work as a medium as well as my personal experience of visiting the Spirit World in 2004 during a near-death experience. It was so profound, that even more than a decade afterward I feel as though I am still learning and discovering things about my time there.

Spiritual Bypassing: Spiritual bypassing is a kind of "toxic positivity" and is a "tendency to use spiritual ideas and practices to sidestep or avoid facing unresolved emotional issues or psychological wounds." The term was first introduced in the 1980s by John Wellwood, a Buddhist teacher, and psychotherapist. Spiritual Bypassing might sound like telling someone who is grieving the loss of a loved one that "everything happens for a reason."

Spiritual tools or Divination tools: anything that is used as an extension of your energy to help aid you in your spiritual practice. I often use tarot cards or oracle cards in my practice and love reading tarot for myself. I find some clients like the familiarity and aesthetic of tarot and oracle cards for intuitive development. They can help us open our senses, but they are a preference and certainly not necessary for Intuitive or mediumship readings.

Telepathy: Mental telepathy refers to the ability to communicate with another person or animal without words. I use telepathy or telepathic communication throughout this book to refer to the way in which I communicate with other humans or Spirit People at times. Sometimes this feels like "hearing thoughts," but for me, telepathy is receiving information through knowing or feeling. I have observed that since many people have this ability and are unaware of it, it is one of my favorite things to point out with new clients.

Vibration: The energetic frequency of a person or place that can be felt by people and animals. The feeling or frequency of our vibration may reflect our thoughts, emotions, behaviors. In mediumship, we refer to "raising our vibration" to meet the higher vibration of those in the Spirit World as we act as a channel to bring through meaningful evidence about the continuity of life.

2

Empaths, Highly Sensitive People & Intuitives

Reimagining Empaths

Psychologists sometimes use "empaths" to refer to an individual's highly attuned nature. They describe empaths as people who are not only sensitive to others' emotions but who often take those emotions on as their own. Emotion researchers define empathy as the ability to sense the emotions of others as well as imagine what someone else is thinking or feeling. New Age spirituality added an element of supernaturalness to the term empath, implying that they have a near-psychic ability to sense emotions.

But labeling people as empaths can become a catch-all term for anyone struggling to understand their highly sensitive or intuitive nature. Many people who come to me identify as an empath—it is often an identity they've adopted or that's been given to them by a spiritual teacher. But I have never found the term to be particularly helpful. As humans, we are all empathic —just as we are all intuitive—and may be affected by the emotional state of the people around us.

I also don't resonate with the "supernatural" aspect of this label—being an empath is the most natural thing for a human to be. Maybe that's why empathy and compassion come easily to most people. The tricky part is how we handle our emotions and set boundaries. While I don't fully resonate with the term empath, I have a deep respect and love for many people who identify with it. This is why I use the term and also why I want to point out some of the ways it may not be helpful to us.

A much more helpful term is "Highly Sensitive Person" (HSP), first introduced in the early 1990s by Psychologist Dr. Elaine Aron. Dr. Aron defined an HSP as "someone who experiences acute physical, mental, or emotional responses to stimuli in their environment and even their own thoughts, emotions, and realizations" *(The Highly Sensitive Person Elaine Aron 1996)*. Oftentimes, when I recommend learning more about being a highly sensitive person to a client who already identifies themselves as a psychic, medium, or empath, they are resistant to this term and see it as a negative label, which really speaks to our conditioning as a society that views sensitivity as a weakness.

I tend to use the terms highly intuitive person (HIP), highly sensitive person (HSP), or empath interchangeably, as they have the same general meaning to me, i.e., someone with a heightened sensitivity to the world around them, including the unseen world. Many of my clients identify as empaths or highly sensitive people and are easily affected by the sounds, smells, and touch of their surroundings.

Mediumship, however, carries with it great sensitivity to not only the world around us but the unseen one. Mediums not only act as a bridge between the Spirit World and the earthly world, but they are also sensitive enough to perceive the Spirit World. Oftentimes, the more we develop our intuition or mediumship, the more sensitive we become to our surroundings. Many intuitive people feel emotions more deeply than others and often need time to process and understand life changes, recharge after interacting with others, or adjust to transitions.

Cara's Story: From Unsure to Empowered

Cara came to me for coaching. Having found herself spending a great deal of time working from home with young children, she was struggling to find a sense of peace and normalcy. During a psychic reading, she had been told she was an empath, and while this helped her make sense of some of the things she'd been experiencing lately, the term seemed to do little to help her. After listening to her speak briefly, I told her that I felt she had natural psychic and mediumship abilities and that I'd like to focus our time together on understanding and developing these. I felt that her intuition had guided her to me and asked her if I could read her energy to validate many of her recent struggles.

This important part of meeting with new clients allows me to demonstrate my intuitive abilities before coaching them on theirs. I set my intention to intuitively sense and feel her energy and began receiving impressions of her past and present experiences, as well as some potential courses for the future.

I told her that I sensed she had a medical trauma in her recent past and knew she had troubling dreams that sometimes-predicted events. I could sense her childhood as a sensitive child, the disconnectedness she felt from her family growing up, and her need to suppress her sensitivity in order to be accepted by her parents. She tended to think in pictures and was a very creative person. In a quest to understand herself, Cara had extensively researched spirituality and different religions and cultures. She felt deeply about the injustices of the world and felt that she could never do or give enough. Sometimes being around harsh or angry people made her feel physically ill. When she met someone, she saw images of their life and knew things about them instantly. But her natural skepticism meant that she could not always make sense of how she knew certain information.

Cara confirmed this was accurate, and the validation seemed to put her immediately at ease. She elaborated on some of the things I'd touched on, and though she was uncomfortable accepting that she had mediumistic abilities, she decided to trust me.

My goals for Cara were to help her understand herself as well as her abilities and then to help her develop them as much as she wanted. Together, we agreed upon a set of goals for our work:

- Demystifying what intuition is and how it manifests for her

- Learning how to separate intuitive messages vs. fear and anxiety
- Learning how to "block" feeling someone else's energy and set energetic boundaries
- Understand the Spirit World better and how spirit guides communicate through various ways
- Understanding the purpose of it all

We met in bi-weekly sessions for a year and Cara began attending my regular Mediumship Practice Circle. As she started to make changes in her life around the ways in which she gave and received energy, nearly all her relationships improved. She began connecting to her spirit guides as well as her own inner knowing and became very in tune with her intuition and psychic messages.

While it was sometimes a struggle, she made many life changes to support her journey. She continues to develop her mediumship and now, a year later, I consider Cara one of the most gifted students I've had the honor to work with.

She has brought me some of the most specific evidence, like receiving words from the Spirit World in another language, and expertly described my great aunt's famous kugel recipe: "She's carrying a dish; it's like a sweet lasagna that tastes like a cinnamon bun." A perfect description of the Jewish comfort food that my Auntie was known for, and which was a staple of my childhood.

While Cara is still unsure of "the purpose of it all," and will sometimes question her abilities, she continues to develop her mediumship and practice. She reports feeling empowered by many of these changes and comforted by her growing understanding of her abilities.

Being "Healed"

There is no "treatment" for being an empath, only a path towards understanding what your own energy feels like, understanding how your body responds to emotions and setting boundaries accordingly.

However, there are a variety of treatments available from the spiritual community which range in effectiveness and ethics. People who experience these "treatments" can feel that their energy and well-being are dependent on them.

Highly empathic people often believe that others can influence their energy without their consent—without even being in the same room. They may believe they have been cursed, that they are carrying trauma from a past life, or that being an empath is like an illness that requires healing. Some of my clients have told me they've spent thousands of dollars on crystals to heal their energy or have paid for someone to remove a curse from them. Others use the less extreme (but also problematic) practice of feeling dependent on regular healing treatments to have someone remove energetic cords or attachments.

Most of the many gifted healers I encounter operate with integrity, but there are certainly practitioners with problematic methods and even a few that take advantage of vulnerable people. Spiritual practices are not highly regulated, so when you are looking for a reputable healer, get recommendations from people before entrusting anyone with your energy.

Years ago, when I experienced Reiki for the first time, I learned a valuable lesson about entrusting someone with my energy. I went for a treatment with a woman who came highly recommended because I was hoping for relief from chronic migraines as well as just being curious about how it would feel to receive a Reiki treatment.

The practitioner first told me that she might go into trance during the healing and said she would try not to slump and smash her head into me during the treatment. Oh?! I thought, trying to dismiss the disturbing thought of her head smashing into mine while I was on the table and hoping that instead of having a serious condition that caused her to faint, she was just trying to show off or embellish her trance abilities. But both ideas were disturbing.

Before the session, I had filled out a several-page-long intake form about all my past surgeries and diagnosis that felt very medical. In it, I disclosed my history of medical trauma and PTSD. When we went over the intake form, she asked intrusive questions about my own work as a medium, even asking how much I paid to rent my office space. She also shared with me that she used to work as a medium herself but had since decided to become a Reiki healer, as it was her "higher calling." When we talked about my migraines, she said regular Reiki treatments could lessen or eliminate my episodes.

I lay on her treatment table for about an hour, slightly tense and hoping she wouldn't drift off and smash her head into mine. Towards the end of the session while I was still laying on my back, she reported that she had "smelled an odor" and "saw a creature that looked like a gargoyle appear." When I questioned her about it, she suggested that perhaps the odor was me and asked if I had an upset stomach. She offered that the gargoyle who had frightened her was one of my spirit guides, adding that her husband had a large and ominous-looking spirit guide that was actually very kind. But as I questioned her about these beliefs, I sensed some animosity from her and began to feel that she was projecting some of her personal fears into this healing session.

As we finished the appointment, she suggested I buy some crystals from her for protection and grounding, which I did. But I left feeling disturbed, and it wasn't until later that day that I started berating myself for not listening to my own intuition telling me that something was not quite right. Obviously, I never returned for another session, and I have since worked with other healers and therapists that I trust and respect.

This kind of work is so varied and unregulated, and over the years I've found that my story was not unique. I'm not sure I believe the practitioner was making it all up—she may actually believe she saw those things. When we are in a meditative state and not operating from our conscious mind, it is common for us to interpret energy as an image, sound, or even smell.

But when we develop our intuition, it's important that we also develop self-awareness and use common sense. Our beliefs and unhealed wounds can interfere with our ability to receive clear information. If someone triggers us to feel something unpleasant—envy for example—we can often interpret that as an ominous feeling or even an image. Since I don't believe the Spirit World is ominous or harmful, I know they would never cause me to suddenly lose consciousness and physically harm myself or someone else. If I did, this belief would very much affect my work. I find that—just like when we fear things we don't understand on the earthly plane—people who have a fear of the Spirit World simply do not understand it.

Understanding Your Energy: Mind, Body, and Spirit

Feeling "drained" by other people is a common reason HSPs or empaths like some of my clients seek healing. I have experienced this feeling, too, and have learned to acknowledge my role in the experience.

It's not possible for another person to supernaturally "take" our energy if we are not giving it.

The act of engaging with someone can be draining because aggravation, anxiety, or having to assert ourselves repeatedly all take energy. When we are in relationships with people who require a lot of our energy, we can start to feel energetically drained and eventually feel disconnected from our spirit. We may then, over time, become accustomed to feeling energetically drained. For instance, I feel drained when I find myself trying to energetically resist someone who is pushing my boundaries. I have to remember to trust myself to stay present and hold those limits. If our boundaries are firm, we can skip the worry and anxiety when they are threatened because we know we can rely on ourselves.

Creating healthy boundaries is often a key part of my intuitive work with clients as they develop their intuition and self-awareness. But to set stable boundaries around our energy, we must first begin to understand what our own energy feels like within the mind, body, and spirit categories.

Mind is the outer layer that contains our thoughts and ideas. When we first sit in meditation, it takes a few minutes for our mind to start to settle down. In those few moments, we have the opportunity to notice our thoughts, which is really helpful in our self-awareness journey. The voice we use to explore these thoughts has already had a huge impact on creating our lived experience.

Imagine having someone especially unkind or strict living inside your head all day! These toxic messages affect how we think about ourselves and our energy. Our world is a much nicer place to be when we speak kindly and with compassion to ourselves. Oftentimes, we develop an inner voice or dialogue that may mirror someone who was critical in our childhood— a parent, a sibling or a classmate that bullied us. Sadly, many people carry on this unhelpful narrative long after childhood, essentially bullying themselves. When we become aware of our mind and our thoughts, we take the first step in addressing negative self-talk.

Your mind and your thoughts are directly related to the next layer: your physical body. Thoughts trigger emotions, and emotions trigger body responses in the physical layer. Through my own experience of having suffered from debilitating migraines since childhood and PTSD as an adult, I know the impact emotions can have on our bodies. I worked with a therapist to address the physical symptoms of my PTSD and now it's easier for me to both make the connections and tell you from personal experience that checking in with yourself—feeling into this emotional and physical body layer—is essential for understanding how your body responds to emotions and developing an awareness of your own energy.

To feel into the essence of the third layer—your spirit—you need to move past the mind and body. I realize words cannot always convey the complexity of how we feel on each of these levels, however I use the word essence—the ultimate nature of something that determines its character—to describe the quality and feeling of our spirit. When we talk about our own essence, this definition helps explain what we are looking for energetically.

How you seem to other people and how you feel to yourself is often in high contrast. When you can start to see and understand yourself as you truly are and feel into your own essence, this can empower you to understand what is your energy, what is not your energy, and how different environments or people affect you.

Your spirit is always available to you. Any time you choose, you can connect to the loving power that is your essence.

I work with a lot of clients who tell me that after a session, they feel they are connecting to the essence of their spirit for the first time. They often describe it as a feeling of reunion or homecoming with themselves, a feeling of being totally free and unlimited.

So, as you explore your mind, body, and spirit, how do you know what your own energy feels like?

The easiest way is to spend time with yourself. Get to know who you truly are beyond any of your roles. Feel beneath the roles of parent, partner, friend, teacher, etc., into who you truly are when you're alone and not presenting your energy to another person.

For me, one of the most healing parts of intuitive work is when I can connect with and validate a client's feelings and energy. Being truly seen by another person can help us shift our perspective and thinking, and oftentimes builds trust and clarity around a situation.

People often tell me I have a calming presence, which is nice to hear but is surprising because that's not how I experience myself—I experience my energy as busy and excited. When I'm in someone else's presence, I clearly know the difference between my energy and theirs. When my clients want to begin developing intuition or understanding energy better, I support them in learning to differentiate their energy from someone else's. Meditation, breath work, and journaling are all helpful tools. But essentially, it comes down to spending time with yourself and observing just being you.

A few years ago, I attended a workshop where I was paired with a medium named Mark for an exercise in which we were instructed to feel into the essence of one another. I didn't know Mark very well at the time, we didn't appear to have much in common and I was skeptical that he was going to be able to tell me much about the essence of my spirit. But as Mark sat across from me and made his connection, I immediately felt relaxed as he started to work and speak.

"I can see that you make other people feel very relaxed and at ease," he said. Other people feel calm when they are in your presence. But that's not how you feel. Your energy is very fast internally. It's not unpleasant!" he added quickly, being cautious not to offend me. "Your essence feels almost like a buzzing energy, always moving and discovering things. It definitely doesn't feel relaxed and serene though."

"Yes," I said. "That is exactly true!" I thanked Mark profusely for his validating reading.

Fast, buzzing, and always moving is exactly how I would describe what it feels to be in my own energy. I have always been in awe when clients and students write to me, saying that I had a calming presence and demeanor. I assumed they were feeling the presence of the Spirit World.

As you get to know how your energy feels, try to remain as self-accepting and non-judgmental as possible. Trust what is coming to you through your intuition. For example, if I had always thought of myself as a very serene and calm person and had been offended by Mark's reading, I would not be able to understand what my own energy feels like. I could go through life blaming my children or my partner for this buzzing energy I feel and try to energetically block them. Or worse, I could go to a healer repeatedly to help me with this "stressful attachment," or bring my family to a healer as well.

Similarly, it's important to be honest with the information we are receiving intuitively. I sensed Mark's hesitation in not wanting to offend me by telling me that I felt surprisingly fast. This is, to a greater degree, common in people new to developing their intuition because our conditioning teaches us not to offend one another. I've had lots of readings from people where they tell me that I feel calm, serene, and confident based on how I appear to them. While there is nothing malicious in this, it can often be invalidating to the recipient. As you begin to work with and trust your intuition, you will begin recognizing when information is coming to you from a place of intuition, and when it is coming from your mind.

Every developing medium has a point in intuitive development where they reach a sense of knowing and develop a greater belief in themself. "Don't give up" is my advice to anyone developing intuition or mediumship, because we never really know how close we are to that knowledge. Many people struggle to find meaning and answers in their intuitive abilities then delay pursuing that exploration out of fear.

The why and how of mediumship and intuitive work may not always be clear, but as you develop your abilities through equal parts discipline and surrender, you will move closer to the truth of who you are. Along with our knowing and our belief in ourselves, we also benefit from having a healthy dose of common sense and a touch of skepticism as we explore our spiritual and intuitive abilities.

You have a right to explore curiosity, passion, and the questions your soul is presenting to you without having all the answers. No one is going to give you permission to lead the kind of life you want to live—you must give that to yourself.

I believe the empathy and deep sensitivity to energy that you experience as a highly sensitive person or empath is a gift. This sensitivity provides greater access to your intuition, and the ability to feel emotions intensely can allow you to experience a more rich and meaningful life. As you learn more about your own energy through self-awareness, and set boundaries that support you, you will be able to better develop your intuition more effectively.

EXERCISE: CONNECTING TO YOUR OWN ENERGY

- Take a moment to find a quiet place where you won't be interrupted. If you'd like, have a notebook or journal and something to write with. Set your intention to connect to yourself and feel your essence.
- In order to feel into your essence—your spirit—you need to move beyond the mind and body. The word "essence" means the ultimate nature of something that determines its character. This definition helps explain what we are looking for energetically when we talk about feeling your own essence. How you seem to other people and how you feel to yourself often contrast, or even conflict. When you start to see and understand yourself as you truly

are and feel into your own essence, it empowers you to discern what is your energy and what is not your energy. You begin to understand how different environments and people are affecting you.

- Take a few slow, gentle breaths and notice how your body starts to relax. As you inhale, let your belly expand in front of you, and as you exhale imagine releasing tension or stress. Trust that your breath will expand your awareness of yourself and expand your consciousness. Repeat this process a few times.
- Allow your breath to fall into its own natural rhythm.
- To relax your body further, start scanning your body from the top of your head down to your toes, noticing any places of tension. As you exhale, allow those places to release. Start to notice how when your *body* is relaxed it is easier for your *mind* to relax.
- You might begin noticing your thoughts coming in and out. It is impossible to have a blank mind. Let your thoughts go by like clouds in the sky. You start to become aware of the separateness of your thoughts. Realize that you are not your thoughts, you are the awareness and consciousness behind your thoughts.

Start to become aware of your true nature, your soul, the eternal part of you that is aligned with your highest good, your inner wisdom. You'll notice that the more you pay attention to this feeling, the bigger it will become.

- Your essence is all-loving. Notice how it feels to connect to this eternal part of you—the part connected to all life and to the source of all life. As you start to become aware of your essence, allow yourself to notice where in your body you feel it. Some people feel their essence in their heart center, and some people feel it in their solar plexus. Some people imagine their essence as a bright light or a color. There is not right or wrong. Simply allow yourself to feel what your essence is *for you*.
- Using your imagination, see your essence—the spiritual you.

With every exhale, your essence becomes bigger filling every fiber of your being. Notice how this light, this color, this power that is all loving, becomes brighter and brighter. Allow it to fill the space in the room around you, expanding beyond and beyond.

- Take a moment to feel into the qualities of you, who you truly are. Notice what your energy feels like without agenda or expectation. Imagine how those in the Spirit World see you—this bright light, the color, the essence of you. Take a few moments to notice any sensations in your body, any emotions that come over you. Simply notice without judgement. Trust that this connection with yourself is always available to you and that you can return to this.
- Journal about your experience.

3

Boundaries

Why We Need Boundaries

Once you gain a deeper understanding of what your own energy feels like and how your emotions feel in your body, you'll need to set boundaries to protect yourself and your energy.

Boundaries are a difficult but essential part of caring for yourself. Saying no without apology or explanation is saying yes to yourself, your energy, and anything you hope to create.

There are many types of boundaries: emotional, physical, intellectual, sexual, and financial. And there are energetic boundaries, visualizations, and intentions that you can use to remain connected to your own energy and not be as affected by others. When I share these psychological and common-sense boundaries in my classes, people are often surprised to have such information presented to them in a spiritual workshop. But I've learned from experience that people who are exploring spiritual development often need to be encouraged to set healthy boundaries. As you become more sensitive to receiving information, you will become more sensitive on other levels as well, so firmer boundaries are often necessary.

The purpose of setting boundaries is to preserve a relationship and aid communication so both parties feel safe. Social media and psychology memes have perpetuated an extreme idea of boundaries. Many New

Age self-help gurus and spiritual teachers offer the most extreme advice on boundary setting: On one end of the spectrum, we have avoidance and complete lack of accountability masquerading as "self-care" and "setting boundaries." On the other end, we have the Spiritualist movement that seems to advocate servitude and endless giving. I've had clients who, without much cause, avoid or refuse to speak to "toxic" or "low vibrational people" in their lives. Many times, because they are simply unable to communicate their need for space and set boundaries, they may permanently abandon a friend in need. Other clients feel they have an obligation to serve so they refuse money for their psychic work or will provide readings beyond their capacity, at a detriment to their health.

When setting boundaries, ask yourself: What do I want to accomplish, and why? While being honest and direct can be difficult, it lets your intuition guide you and does less harm to those you love.

Highly sensitive people/empaths usually struggle with emotional boundaries in relationships. To feel safe as an HSP, you likely had to shut down your sensitivity and intuition in the past. Creating a safe environment in your life now will help as you open your intuition back up. This can mean setting boundaries with people who have questioned or shut down your sensitivity in the past—even people you love. It can mean acknowledging what you need to feel safe and comfortable.

When we are not under stress or fear of judgment, it's easier to feel into our intuition. This is likely going to take time and practice, especially if you had to shut down or disconnect from emotions in the past to survive

How to Begin Setting Boundaries

When you set boundaries, aim to establish ones that allow you to live fully in the present moment and are aligned with your intuition. Healthy boundaries help conserve your energy.

This can be difficult with the people we love. Remember that even though you can feel someone's emotions, *you are not responsible for fixing them.*

Setting boundaries with people you love may sound like:

"That's not something I want to talk about."

"I won't have time for that this week."

"This makes me uncomfortable, let's do something else."

"This topic is off-limits for me."

"I'm not always able to respond immediately because I'm limiting the time I spend on my devices/social media."

"I need some time to myself, please don't interrupt me."

When setting boundaries with people we love, I recommend replacing the word "but" with "and." When we use the word "but" after our first statement, people usually don't hear the rest of what we say.

Instead of saying "I love talking to you, but I need space right now." We can say "I love talking to you *and* I need space right now." Or instead of, "I enjoy our visits, but I need you to call and ask if it's a good time before stopping by" try "I enjoy our visits, *and* I need you to call and ask if it's a good time before stopping by."

This makes it easier for people to hear the first part of what we've said and doesn't negate our first statement to them.

As you develop your intuition, setting boundaries will become a way to practice self-love, and like any practice, it will take time and will be ongoing. This is difficult in the beginning, and not everyone will respect or understand your boundaries. That's okay. It is not our job to manage other people's emotional reactions. Once you begin setting boundaries and trust your intuition around setting them, you will develop confidence in the process

When creating boundaries, it's helpful to clearly establish your intentions and set them for yourself. This way, you get clear on both why you are setting boundaries and the benefits of this practice.

Here are some statements of intention you may want to use as you begin to practice setting boundaries:

"In saying no to something that is not aligned, I make space for something new."

"I am intentional with whom and what I share my energy with."

"My feelings do not require an apology."

"When I say no to someone and they get upset, that does not mean I should have said yes."

"I set boundaries that allow me to live fully in the present moment as much as possible."

Of course, sometimes we will need to let go of a relationship with someone who is not receptive to our boundaries or refuses to honor them. Sometimes, not giving any more of our energy to this person IS the boundary. This loss can be painful. Here is an intention I have used to help process my feelings over the loss of a friend, an opportunity, or after a breakup:

"I let go of what is not meant to stay.

I allow any feelings of loss and release them.

I remain open and curious to receive what's next."

In my intuitive coaching work, my ultimate goal for someone who identifies as an empath is empowerment. By providing clear answers and sharing my own experiences, I hope to inspire people to feel confident in their own choices and understand that being an empath is not a life sentence to "feel the emotions of others."

I see many HSP/empaths who have been in relationships with people who are unloving and rely on the HSP/empath to fulfill their emotional needs—essentially taking energy from them and using them as a source to satisfy their need for admiration and attention.

Oftentimes, HSP/empathic people put the needs of others above their own. In an attempt to feel loved, validated or to heal childhood wounds and repair their self-worth, they try to heal the uncaring, selfish, or even abusive and narcissistic people in their lives. But the more energy they pour into these relationships, the more power and control the uncaring or narcissistic partner, friend, or family member acquires.

We don't need to accept that other people are going to leave us feeling drained. If we learn to become familiar with and stay connected to the essence of our own energy—and we understand how people affect us emotionally and energetically— we can set boundaries that support our well-being and cultivate inner peace. I learned this lesson the hard way.

My Story: From Seeking Belonging to Setting Boundaries

When I was a senior in high school, my family moved from Florida, where we had lived for three years, back to our home state of Massachusetts. Because I was in serious jeopardy of not having enough credits to graduate, I convinced my parents to allow me to stay in Florida. They agreed to let me live with some friends of theirs for the few months left before graduation. I planned to stay in Florida and attend a local college. At the time I had a new boyfriend, Conner, and it was exciting to me to be on my own in another state.

Conner was a few years older than me and worked as an art dealer in Miami. We had gone to high school together, although he had never acknowledged me in school except to tease me a few times about being so quiet. When we met up again my senior year, I was shocked that he started paying attention to me and even more surprised when he asked me out on a date. He came to my parents' house the morning of our date to bring me a gift—a red dress that he had wrapped and asked me to wear that night. It wasn't anything like my other clothes, and when I opened the box, I just stared at the dress in disbelief trying to imagine how this red piece of fabric was going to look covering my body.

I tried to seem appreciative and excited but all I could think to say was, "What kind of shoes am I supposed to wear with this?"

"Do you have red shoes?" he asked.

I owned only one pair of dress shoes that I wore to my hostess job, and I felt like they didn't even belong in the same universe as this dress. They definitely weren't red. I skipped my last two classes of the day and drove to the mall to buy the cheapest, most uncomfortable pair of red shoes I could find, then went home to put on the dress and the shoes. I felt completely naked. I stared at myself in the mirror for as long as I could, trying to get up the confidence I would need to leave the house dressed like this.

I couldn't wear a bra with this dress, but because of my eating disorder, I didn't need one. I ended up throwing on a black cardigan at the last minute and running out the door. Because I had no experience setting boundaries, it never occurred to me that I could simply choose to wear something else. I mistook another person wanting to control me as a deeper connection.

Conner met me in the driveway and insisted on coming back inside to meet my parents. I watched squeamishly as he casually asked my dad questions about his business and complimented my mom on her decorating, saying things like, "I love this granite" and asking her specific questions about the fabric of our curtains.

"So, what do you do for a living, Curtis?" he asked my dad as he leaned back against the kitchen counter. He seemed so comfortable in our house, like he owned the place.

"I sell cars," my dad answered in his thick Boston accent.

"Cows?" Conner asked, raising an eyebrow. *He was making fun of my dad.*

"Cars," my dad answered, emphasizing the R.

My dad wasn't exactly selling cars—we had moved to Florida so he could run the largest Ford dealership in the United States. But he seemed amused by whatever game Conner was playing with him, and the two of them bantered back and forth for a few more excruciating minutes.

We finally left and Conner drove us to a restaurant on Miami Beach. During the drive, he explained all about the history of the place, what they had on the menu, and told me what I should order. I had been there a few times with my parents, but I didn't mention that because I didn't want to take away from his excitement. I listened quietly as he talked about himself for the next few hours. He didn't mind that I hardly spoke.

I tried my best to follow along with everything he was saying about his family, his art dealing business, and his investment properties. We were sitting outside, and I was glad I had my sweater on. "You look great in that dress." he said, "I should buy you more clothes."

It was exciting to be the focus of Conner's attention, so I just shrugged and continued trying to hold in place whatever "this" was that he thought looked great. He seemed confident and successful, and having his approval and attention gave me a feeling of belonging that I had struggled to find since the sexual assault I experienced as a younger teen.

Since I had never processed that trauma, I was seeking validation and acceptance. The man who sexually assaulted me had criticized me as he was assaulting me, adding another layer of shame to my trauma. I had internalized his comments about my body, my mannerisms, and the tone of my voice, and believed them to be true. Each time Conner complimented me, I felt an empty space inside me being filled.

I didn't realize at the time that I was capable of filling myself with love and belonging, that I belonged first to myself.

We continued seeing each other for another six months. Conner shared a house with a roommate, and it didn't take long after my parents moved for me to start staying over at his house on a regular basis. Eventually, I moved in with him.

He never did buy me more clothes, but he didn't need to. I anticipated what he wanted me to wear and slowly began dressing that way. In the beginning, I enjoyed doing things and dressing in ways that he would like. But his approval became increasingly harder to obtain, and I began changing my behavior to keep him from criticizing me or becoming angry.

I started to anticipate his mood swings or what he expected me to say and do, which became more difficult as his business started failing. I was waitressing full time and made a decent income, but when I tried to contribute financially, he got angry. He didn't like the uniform my job required— jean shorts and an oversized navy-blue t-shirt with a fish bones logo. Eventually, I started changing my clothes in the bathroom before leaving work so that when I came home, he wouldn't get upset when he saw me.

I started to feel like my presence in his life was harming him somehow and didn't know quite how to exist without offending him. He often complained that I was too quiet. He said it upset his friends that I didn't talk to them and although his family seemed to like me, he said they thought I was stuck up because I wasn't friendlier. "Could you just be normal?" he'd ask me before we would go anywhere. It became really clear to me after living with Conner for a few months that I absolutely could not be normal, and I had no idea how to do or be the right thing in most situations.

My mind was constantly occupied with how he was feeling, and most of the time I felt disconnected from my body. Some mornings I would have the house to myself, but I couldn't relax because I knew that Conner could come home at any moment. There was nowhere in the house that I could be alone—I had no privacy at all.

One day, Conner and his roommate took me with them to adopt a pit bull mix from a local shelter near the Everglades. Daisy had been neglected and abused, but she was still a puppy and very spirited. I began taking her for walks during the day and training her. I looked forward to spending time with her alone, which no one seemed to mind because she had so much energy, my attention and our walks kept her occupied. Other than those times with Daisy, I felt disconnected from my spirit and didn't feel like myself. I didn't know or recognize my own energy. My essence was just trying to survive.

I had become a blank slate, tiptoeing around, trying to exist without being noticed. When my high school graduation day came, the whole event felt anticlimactic because my family was not around, and I was grateful to have Conner with me. The plan was, Conner would drive me to the ceremony and then we'd have a party at his house afterwards. Since my parents had moved back to Massachusetts months earlier (and there was so much uncertainty around whether I would graduate) my dad was the only one planning to fly in. He'd attend the ceremony then Conner and I would have an early dinner with him before he flew home. Even though I wouldn't know any of the people at Conner's party afterwards, I liked the idea of a party because it seemed like a normal high school thing to do.

When the day came though, Conner seemed stressed and nervous. He was angry with me about not helping enough for the party. He accused me of being too concerned about the graduation. And instead of driving me to the ceremony as planned, he insisted I stand in the kitchen and listen to his complaints. I ended up driving myself and arrived late, in a panic.

When I walked out on stage, I looked for Conner, but I didn't see him anywhere. He never showed up to dinner afterwards and I spent the entire dinner with my dad, worrying about what Conner's reaction would be. I arrived home hours later to a house party full of strangers, some sleeping on the furniture, some gathered in groups on the lawn. I crept upstairs and tried to fall asleep alone in a bedroom which wasn't really mine. Afraid to lock the door in case Conner wanted to go to bed and afraid to leave it unlocked in case a stranger walked in, I decided to leave the door unlocked.

As I lay there, I tried to question how I felt about the situation. I tried to remember why I had wanted this relationship in the first place, and what about it had made me happy. I stared intently at the door, imagining scenarios of who could walk through it and what might happen. The relationship that had once given me a feeling of belonging now left me feeling that I didn't belong anywhere. Ultimately, the tension of watching the door kept me from accessing my own anger and sadness about Conner not showing up for me, and I fell asleep to the sounds of the party downstairs.

A few weeks later, Conner borrowed a friend's convertible and we drove to a restaurant where his sister worked. I was underage, but he said he wanted me to be able to drink with him. He was upset because a friend of his had started taking antidepressants and Conner felt this was affecting his friend's personality, turning him into "an asshole." I don't remember much of that night, only bits and pieces. He had a lot to drink, and I didn't want him to drive, and we argued about it. He eventually convinced me that he was okay, becoming calm and agreeable.

Once he got behind the wheel, though, something changed. He became angry that I had questioned his ability to drive and started speeding and driving erratically on purpose. I must have shown how relieved I was when we finally pulled into our neighborhood, because he got even more upset. He started slamming his foot on the break and yelling at me at the same time. He hit the break so hard that I would fly forward, almost hitting my head on the dashboard. The more afraid I became, the more he seemed to enjoy it. I tried to be whatever he needed me to be in that moment, as always, and as always, it didn't work. I became still, quiet, agreeable. I tried to disappear.

The next morning, I woke up disoriented and sick. My head was pounding from the drinks the night before and my body was sore everywhere. As I got up and walked to the bathroom, I caught a glimpse of myself in the mirrored closet door. Across my chest were bright blue horizontal marks where the seat belt had done its job holding me in place. I looked down at my toes and saw flecks of dried blood with dirt on top and my toenails were chipped and broken from putting my feet out to break my fall in my sandals. A dried leaf was lodged in my hair. I thought I must have fallen trying to get back to the house, but I couldn't remember.

When I looked at my face in the mirror, a complete stranger looked back at me. I felt an intense wave of nausea as I whispered to myself, "Who are you?"

A few weeks later, I was rushing to get to work. I still loved my job—it was a great place to work except that it was a forty-five-minute drive from Conner's house. I couldn't find my key, so I left out the back slider, knowing he would be home soon. About fifteen minutes into my drive, he paged me 911. This was before cell phones, so I had to decide: keep driving to work at the restaurant and barely make it on time, pull over and find a payphone to call him and be late, or turn around and drive back home to see what he wanted and be very late for work. Something made me choose option three.

The people I worked with—especially some of the older women who worked there—were already concerned about me. One lady, Di, had commented the week before that Conner was "sucking the life out of me," which had made me angry at the time. But now I was grateful because I felt that I could just explain that we'd had a fight and I knew she'd be supportive. I turned around and drove home. Conner was in the driveway, and he looked shocked to see me drive up.

"Jesus Christ, you didn't have to come back," he said.

"I wanted to see why you paged me," I answered.

"You left the door unlocked," he said. "I told you not to do that, it's so disrespectful."

I thought about telling him that I couldn't find my key, and that I knew he would be home any minute anyway, but that didn't seem like it would be helpful, given the mood he was in. "I'm late for work," I said. "I drove back here because I thought it was an emergency."

"Don't blame this on me," he said, looking disgusted. "I didn't ask you to come back here. I don't even want you here." He seemed more upset than usual. He was at least ten feet away from me in the driveway, but I could feel his body vibrating in anger. Our next-door neighbor who had been watering his grass put down the hose and went inside.

Suddenly my body felt numb and tingling all the way to my toes. I felt something shifting in the atmosphere around me. It felt like something was about to happen. I made eye contact with Conner, something I rarely did anymore. "You don't want me here?" I asked, surprised at how calm and steady my voice sounded.

He stared right into my eyes, "I don't care if you stay or if you go," he said with a chilling smile that reminded me of his expression when he was about to slam his foot on the brakes and send me flying into the dashboard.

"I don't love you anymore," he said, still making eye contact with me in a way that made me feel unsafe. Then he turned and confidently walked back into the house like he was expecting me to follow him. I watched him walk in the front door and leave the door open behind him.

Something within me took over in that moment in the driveway. Without thinking, I calmly got back into my car and started to drive away. I felt like someone else. As my hands gripped the steering wheel, it felt like they were covered by someone else's hands. In my peripheral vision I saw the flash of a man's face in black and white. It felt as though he was sitting next to me in the passenger seat, in quiet support of my decision. I had the distinct feeling that if I was to change my mind or stop driving away from the house, this man would intervene somehow. That was comforting to me, yet at the same time, I could not make sense of it.

I drove to a payphone and called my mother to tell her some of what had happened. I tried to sound like I was crying because I felt that I should be crying at this point. The truth is, though, I wasn't feeling anything. It was like I was operating from some place deep inside me without any thought or emotion. My mom immediately offered to buy me a plane ticket. "Go right to the airport," she begged.

I agreed. I put more change in the phone, called my work, and told them Conner and I had had a fight and that I was going home to Boston. I was sorry I couldn't say goodbye, but I needed to go to the airport right now. Di came onto the phone to quickly wish me goodbye. She seemed happy and relieved, further validating my choice.

Not that I needed validation at that point. Nothing was going to stop me from getting on that plane—not even Conner driving to the airport and sitting at the gate crying on my lap and begging me not to leave, which he did. My dad hired someone to fly down to Florida and drive my car back to Boston with as many things as he could get from the house. I didn't call anyone besides my job to say goodbye—I didn't have anyone else to call. In what was considered my final act of disrespect, I forgot to even say goodbye to Conner's roommate, and we never spoke again.

In one moment, I left my entire existence, my college plans, my relationship, and our dog without a thought. I acted on this feeling, this knowing that I needed to go. It wasn't what he had said about not loving me, it was that I could feel how much he wanted to hurt me—maybe even kill me. And I had this knowing that if I followed him into the house, if I didn't go to the airport right then, I would not be safe. Since the beginning of our relationship, I had dismissed every instinct of fear and intuition that I'd had. Now it felt both freeing and terrifying to acknowledge and act on my feelings.

I never told anyone the reason why I left because I felt embarrassed that I had allowed myself to be completely consumed by the relationship. Instead, I focused on what he'd said about not loving me. "I couldn't be with someone who doesn't love me," I'd say, but it wasn't that simple. For so long I had denied the reality that I was in a relationship with someone who enjoyed hurting me, that I didn't even know how I felt. All my energy went into surviving, and I felt completely disconnected from my mind, body, and spirit.

After I moved back home, I found a job waitressing at a local Italian restaurant. The people were warm and friendly, and they were understaffed, so they were thrilled to have someone who liked to work a lot. And I was so grateful to be in a warm, inviting atmosphere, that I said I'd work six nights a week. It felt like a family to me and a lot of the older professional people who worked there as their second job seemed to respect that I was quiet and shy. Eventually, their kindness earned my trust and I started to open up to everyone and find my voice.

I wish I could say that I never saw Conner again, but we saw each other a few more times. He said he was devastated after I left, and he flew to Boston twice wanting to get back together. Since I had started to heal and develop some boundaries, I wasn't as vulnerable to his attempts to control or manipulate me. I also had the security of living with my family, and I had started to imagine what I might want to do with my life. I enrolled in community college and decided I'd like to be a nurse. My high school grades were not enough to get into a nursing program, but I had gotten an impressive score on the SATs, so the college advisor suggested that after a year in community college, and with decent grades, I could transfer into another program. Most of the classes were small, so it was easier for me to pay attention. If I needed help for difficult classes, I went for tutoring after-school. For the first time, I started getting good grades and I felt more confident in my abilities.

Two years later, I planned to see Conner. I drove to Miami from Boston with some friends, and he convinced me to stay with him for a weekend. On the way to Miami, we stopped to visit a friend. Scott was a Marine stationed on a naval base in Kings Bay, Georgia. When we met up with him and a bunch of guys from his unit in the parking lot of a hotel, they were waiting for their one friend who was responsible enough to have a credit card for the hotel room. I felt annoyed sitting on the pavement in the hot sun like a child—I had my own credit card and felt this was ridiculous.

Then I looked up and saw Mike (now my ex-husband) about twenty feet away, walking towards us. Something made me stand up, and out of the periphery of my mind I saw the same scene in black and white: Mike was walking towards me, but he was dressed in a suit and standing someplace that was familiar, but I couldn't quite place. As I tried to make sense of it, I realized it was the country club where my aunt and uncle had gotten married a few years ago. Then I had another, much more surprising thought: I am going to marry this guy. Mike walked straight up to the group of guys, completely ignored all the girls sitting there, and started explaining the rules of staying in the hotel: it was his credit card, they better not damage anything, they were on a "36," which meant that they only had thirty-six hours off before they had to report back into the base.

"Okay, Corporal Wags," some of them groaned.

Scott slapped him on the back and said, "I'm glad you came. You really need to relax buddy!"

Corporal Wags stiffened and gave them all a stern look. Clearly, this guy was their boss who had come along to keep everyone out of trouble and make sure they were safe. Even when he pulled one of the younger guys aside and it looked like he was having a serious talk with him, it seemed that he really cared about his men.

The next day, we all went to the beach and my friend got the worst sunburn I've ever seen. We decided it wouldn't be safe (and definitely not comfortable) for her to drive from Georgia to Miami. Mike kindly offered for us to stay in his apartment, generously handing over the keys as he wouldn't be staying there because he had to go back to work on base.

I instantly felt safe in his presence, he seemed kind and genuine. We made plans to see each other again the following month and he asked if I'd fly down to meet him at Disney World.

I never called Conner to tell him we weren't coming to Miami. The next time we spoke was two years later when he called me around his own birthday. When he asked what I was doing, I told him I was married and had just had a baby boy. He was quiet for a moment.

"Are you breastfeeding him?" he asked.

"Ummm, yes," I said, genuinely confused by the question.

"I'm glad," he said.

"Why?" I asked.

"Because my mom never breastfed me because she's too selfish."

He asked me questions about Mike—mostly about his military service—and I happily answered all his questions. I told him how Mike had been awarded a Navy Achievement Medal for his service in Iraq. I said how happy we were.

What I didn't mention was that I had just almost died during childbirth, that I didn't have the strength to stand up and hold my own baby, or that my baby wasn't even with me—he was still in the NICU. As I listened to Conner talk about his new business venture, I closed my eyes and imagined him sitting on a beach somewhere far away. I mentally closed the curtain on that image and let it fade until he was gone. That was the last time we spoke.

Sometimes not giving someone any more of our energy is the boundary.

EXERCISE: SETTING ENERGETIC BOUNDARIES (PROTECTING YOUR ENERGY)

- Sit quietly for a few moments in a place you won't be disturbed
- Have a journal and something to write with if you wish
- Set your intention for this exercise and write it down if you wish. Your intention can be simply one word like "peace" or "calm" or "protection," or it can be more specific. The more specific your intention, the more specific your results will be.

For example, if you are concerned about other people draining your energy, a good intention would be: "I am intentional with whom and what I share my energy."

If you are going to be around someone who feels challenging to you or in an uncomfortable situation, a good intention would be "I am vital, strong, and protected by my inner knowing."

- Start by taking three deep cleansing breaths. As you inhale through your nose and the air fills your lungs, feel the power of your intention (strength, vitality, love) filling you. As you exhale slowly through your mouth, allow anything that is not needed (fear, self-doubt) to be released.

- Allow your breath to fall into a natural rhythm. Focus your mind on your breath until you feel a sense of calm or well-being and start to sense a connection with your essence. Imagine what it looks like energetically. How do you appear to the Spirit World? Is it a swirl of color or a bright light? Focus on this image or idea of your spiritual essence. Now imagine your essence fully surrounding you for a few moments. Notice the edge of your essence—your light or color. With your imagination, make the edges of your energy impenetrable. No one can enter this light surrounding you without your permission.

- When you feel that you've fully visualized this, state your intention again.

- Journal about this experience if you wish.

4

Finding Alignment

How Intuition Helps Us Find Alignment

Alignment means to bring into a line or proper position with something else. In the car business, it refers to the suspension that is responsible for connecting a vehicle to its wheels. The angles of the wheels, the camber, toe, and caster all need to be adjusted properly so they make the right contact with the road, allowing you to drive straight, getting safely and easily where you need to go. If the alignment is off, you'll know it because your car will pull to the right or left. There could be a vibration in the steering wheel, making you hold on tightly to keep your wheel straight. If you've ever experienced this, you know it's not a pleasant way to drive. If we drive with a car that's out of alignment for too long, the tires suffer premature wear and tear and unnecessary damage.

Yes, you can get where you're going. But depending on how badly off the alignment is, it's hard to relax or think about anything else besides the fact that your car is constantly pulling to one side of the road. You may find yourself over-correcting and exhausted from all the effort.

When we talk about alignment in a spiritual sense, we are talking about being in alignment with our spiritual values and true essence. Our conscious and unconscious mind, our physical body, and our breath need to be aligned with our truth, or we will likely feel a sense of discomfort. We may feel like we're struggling to stay on the road.

At some point as adults, most of us develop a set of values, beliefs, and ideas that help us live in alignment. We begin to form ideas of what is wrong and right, and what it looks like to live a good life. For example, most people believe that they need to work hard and make sacrifices to be successful. Through our conditioning—in our families and in society—most of us have this thought reinforced throughout our lifetime. Such recurring thoughts eventually become beliefs.

By the time we reach adulthood, most of us are prepared to suffer and work hard for what we want. While we may value feeling rested and spending time with our family and friends, our belief that we must work hard to be successful will shape the way we behave and the choices we make. We may, for example, believe we are making the right choice for our family when we choose a higher-paying job with better benefits even if it requires us to work long hours, be away from our family, and sacrifice our health.

I was born in 1982 and grew up with heavy messaging of, "You can be anything you want to be." Many people of my generation who grew up in middle-class families in the United States had this belief constantly reinforced through parents and teachers.

This conditioning exposes us to constant comparison with our peers. Capitalism and consumerism teach us that we must always have and be more, contributing to generations of kids believing they should be able to be anything they want and blaming themselves for not feeling fulfilled and successful.

The problem with this belief is that it puts emphasis on achievement rather than self-development. The idea that we can be anything suggests we should be more and shouldn't stop because "the sky's the limit." It suggests that we are not enough as we are, that we need to become something else to earn love, respect, and belonging.

Through our conscious choice, we can alter our thoughts, beliefs, and values. Science has shown that through sustained practice and behavioral changes we can rewire the neural pathways in our brain to form new beliefs that support how we'd like our life to feel.

For example, someone who grew up in an emotionally neglectful home and has low self-worth can, over time, choose self-affirming thoughts that build their self-esteem. When we put a self-love practice in place—especially through self-development and/or with a professional therapist—we can greatly improve the quality of the thoughts and beliefs we have about ourselves, ultimately improving the overall quality of our lives.

The idea that we can choose our thoughts and shape our reality is not new. Most ancient religions speak of these teachings: The Buddha famously said that thoughts make us what we are, Jesus spoke of our limitless power to create, and Marcus Aurelius wrote in 180 AD that "your life is what your thoughts make it."

These teachings are often used to encourage us to choose what we'd like to have and then achieve it by aligning ourselves with what we've chosen. While there is nothing wrong with this way of thinking, the emphasis tends to be on what we "want." People read books like *The Secret* in hopes of manifesting financial abundance or a love interest.

What's missing for me in these teachings, is that they skip the spiritual and self-development that allows us to know our truth. Most people want to feel good, so we try to manifest things we think will make us feel good—a beach house for example. If everyone who read *The Secret* (Rhonda Byrne 2006) decided instead to manifest self-love and spiritual abundance, the world would be a far different place.

I believe we need to invite our intuition into the process of alignment because the

truth is, we are all inherently worthy of love, respect, and belonging. We don't need to earn it.

I believe our purpose is to discover who we are and to fully be that person. We can't and shouldn't be anything we want, nor align ourselves with a monetary or even a spiritual goal. As much as my life has led me through extraordinary circumstances to become a psychic medium, I don't believe that is my singular purpose in life. I've met many spiritual teachers who talk about their purpose being to serve the Spirit World, and that's a noble idea. Yet I believe everything we do serves the Spirit World, and that our purpose is not to be or do one thing. Rather, our purpose is to discover who we are and to feel our own aliveness as much as possible in every moment we are here. Sometimes this feels like being bored, angry, sad, joyful, or envious. Our purpose cannot be chased by us or quantified by the amount of happiness we feel or do not feel.

Since my near-death experience in 2004, a recurring thought that seems to come from the Spirit World is, "you are meant to be here." At times, this thought felt punitive to me—patronizing and sometimes even cruel. Though I am still discovering the meaning of my near-death experience, what I've come to understand or interpret from its lesson is that my purpose is to just be here as my full self.

Spirit has reinforced this understanding in many ways. However, the deep feeling of the message comes from within me. My intuition is my guide and my greatest navigator in discovering this sense of purpose.

I've come to believe that we need to invite our intuition into the process of alignment.

Things flow more easily when you live in alignment with your intuition, although it looks different for everyone. If you are living your life in alignment with your conditioning and not your intuition, things may look great on the outside. You can appear successful, happy, healthy, and financially secure by choosing partners, jobs, and friends based on what you *think* you should have and not at all aligned with what you feel is right for you.

When you start to develop and trust your intuition, it can be challenging to move away from external validation and towards your own internal strength and self-acceptance. Whether it's not seeing our monthly numbers on an excel spreadsheet to know we have achieved something, or not gaining approval from certain people in our lives, it can feel like a loss.

Starting to rely on your body as a powerful indicator of your emotional needs can help guide you in this process. The need to rest, move away from certain people and environments, change behaviors and thinking patterns, will all be felt in the body first. For many of my clients, the concept of trusting their body feels foreign. Our conditioning tells us that productivity is far better than rest, that we should be unbothered by noise, crowds, fluorescent lights, and the cleaning product that gives us a headache.

When we are not in alignment, we feel it in our body. Our body is like an antenna for energy and information—it's one of the most trustworthy barometers of alignment. Many highly sensitive and intuitive people have been living in a state of anxiety or unrest for so long, it's easy for them to miss the body cues that tell them they're not in alignment with their purpose and intuition. Intuition speaks to you calmly from your center, a place of love. It does not speak from fear, and it will never lie to you.

While it's difficult to explain what living a life in alignment with intuition looks like, it's easy to describe what it feels like and to recognize it. As you develop your values instead of relying on your conditioning, and begin to understand intuition, you also begin to discover the truth of who you are. Then, what your soul wants to express becomes the basis for this alignment.

My Story: A Forced Realignment

When I was in my career as a finance manager, my values were to take care of my family, earn a good living, to appear healthy and in control of my emotions. I put these core values above all else. Because I had aligned myself with these goals, I had to put the parts of myself that did not uphold these goals away for years. I couldn't show how sensitive I was to the world around me nor have emotional reactions to my experiences. I would push myself to work beyond my physical limits and deprive my body of adequate food, water, and rest to achieve my goals. At that time, I was actually proud of these sacrifices because this is also something our society reinforces through conditioning. We see being productive and financially successful as a great achievement, even when it comes at the cost of our health and well-being.

Like many people, I was forced to realign my life.

One day, my son was hospitalized, and to go see my doctor, I left a full schedule of clients waiting. I felt unable to speak, so when the doctor came into the room, I handed him my phone open to the notes section where I had written:

> "My son is having a mental health crisis. I need to be at my strongest for my family right now, but I am afraid I may be having some type of a nervous breakdown. I have been trying to meditate, take breaks at work, go to my support group, and I go to weekly counseling. I can't exercise because I am recovering from walking pneumonia.
>
> "The problem is, sometimes when I am not thinking about anything, I suddenly feel very afraid and start to shake and feel nauseous. One night last week when I closed my eyes to go to sleep, I started to feel my heart race. I thought I was having a heart attack. Even though I know what a panic attack is, I really thought I was going to die. I have a diagnosis of PTSD from 10 years ago, but this felt much worse than any panic attacks I've had before. I took an old prescription I had, and I was able to get through the attack after about 30 minutes.
>
> "Last Thursday I had my sister drive me to urgent care because it happened while I was at work. The doctor there wrote me a prescription which I have now had to take several times to control the panic. I don't like the way it makes me feel but it works quickly. I feel very out of control and not connected to my body at times. I can't focus at work and I am having a hard time eating and sleeping. I feel nauseous most of the day. I have nightmares most every night."

My doctor, although sympathetic, did not have much to offer besides recommending that I take time off work and focus on my health.

A few weeks later my son came home, and things began to improve. At the same time, I had begun connecting to the Spirit World more and made the decision to let go of our full-time nanny so I could be more involved at home and have time to develop my mediumship. Lately I began to experience visions with increasing frequency and intensity, and I needed time and space to explore and understand what was happening.

I rented a small office space so that I would have a place to explore what was happening and I began offering free mediumship readings to the public, which went well. Being able to use my abilities to help others and cooperate with The Spirit World was a relief. My mediumship work felt true to who I was, while being a finance manager felt increasingly less true.

Strange occurrences began happening at work that made it more difficult to focus. Suddenly, clients who had no knowledge of my mediumship abilities were coming into my finance office telling me they had lost loved ones, even showing me photographs of them. When I closed my eyes, I saw faces flashing before me and I felt my own deceased loved ones around me with increasing clarity. I would be working late at night and hear them speaking to me. On several occasions, I felt my grandmother take my hand. And I started to psychically see and know things about my colleagues. The Universe seemed to be sending me signs at every turn.

That month, I also began to notice hawks everywhere I went, swooping so low over my car that I could see the white feathers of their underbelly up close. I asked the Spirit World to please let me know what the meaning of these hawks were, and a thought entered my mind that hawks have excellent vision, they clearly see the bigger picture and take action. A few moments after this thought, a hawk crashed into my office window and died. I felt that this was the sign I had asked for.

The following week, my boss gave me the ultimatum: either return to working sixty hours a week or lose my job in finance altogether. It was an easy decision—there was no way I could continue living as I had been. I quit my job as a finance manager and began building my professional mediumship practice

Living in alignment with my truth felt so freeing that once I had a sense of it, I was unlikely to make concessions that would bring me out of alignment. And I quickly learned that when I made decisions that did not support my alignment, I felt "off" or "wrong". I knew I had been denying a part of myself and was compelled to correct it.

In a similar way, your truth and understanding are going to evolve and change over time. Being in alignment takes on-going dedication to yourself. When you are presented with new information, or the truth of yourself, it is natural to resist. Our minds want comfortability and to keep us safe. That's why breaking or starting a new habit can be difficult, and it is the same with intuition. We need to continue to build the relationship with ourselves, with our intuition, if we want to be in alignment.

As you grow and evolve so will your trust in yourself, in your intuition, and in the Spirit World. Being in alignment is not a destination to be reached, but a feeling you may become familiar with. Likewise, being out of alignment is easy to recognize. Too often, though, we resist admitting this feeling because as intuitive people we know it means significant change and letting go of people and things that feel comfortable. If we could have faith that our soul is pushing us to grow for a reason—and that our discomfort would ultimately lead to positive changes and living in our truth—we could evolve more quickly and easily. Having such faith is a practice as well.

My Story: When Alignment Came Calling (Again)

After I left my work at the car dealership and started my mediumship practice, I finally started to feel aligned in my work. Everything in that area of my life felt easy, right, and comfortable. My work was fulfilling and exciting, and I felt a sense of peace and ease that I had never had before.

However, there was still a big, unaligned piece of my life. As I became more willing to live authentically and honestly, I became more uncomfortable with this truth. The discomfort was pushing me to re-align again.

During the summer of 2020, my ex-husband and I rented a beach house with our two boys over the Fourth of July. By this time, he and I had spoken frequently about the fact that I was gay. Our current plan was to stay married and living together, coparenting the way we were and not disrupt our sons' lives in any way. Intellectually, I felt it made perfect sense that we stay together. We also knew that we were great friends, and after working together in the car business for fifteen years, we were happy to be able to support each other in the new businesses we had each started two years earlier. We kept our plans to vacation at the beach house, but what I thought would be a time to connect with the kids and relax ended up pushing me to face the fact that I was not really living as my full self.

The quaint beach cottage surrounded by crisp, cheery hydrangeas was in stark contrast to my emotional state. I walked on the beach at 5 a.m. every morning and stared out into the ocean, feeling profoundly lonely. The sunshine felt wrong, like a spotlight illuminating my emptiness, and the decisions I needed to make took up all the space in my mind. I tried to talk myself out of what I was feeling. I reasoned with myself that I loved Mike; he was my family. Mike and I met in our twenties and in lots of ways, we'd grown up together. We'd always been honest and accepting of one another and that had held our relationship together over the past seventeen years. It was hard for me to imagine a life without him, and I didn't want to cause my children any pain. I wanted everything to remain comfortable for everyone. The problem was, I had a growing discomfort and knowing that things were going to have to change.

That night while I was getting dinner ready, Mike announced to the boys that he was going to go "man the grill." I rolled my eyes and the boys groaned and giggled as we began the comical process of explaining that grills have no gender. Mike did not seem to understand this concept, and at one point in exasperation I said, "Do you ever think we are just not compatible?"

"Oh, I *know* we're not compatible!" he grinned at me. We all laughed and enjoyed the rest of our night together, but I couldn't shake my feeling of dread. I was so afraid of disappointing the kids and causing them pain—how would they react when they found out their parents were not right for one another in a significant way?

On day three of our vacation, I texted a friend sarcastically typing, "I think we may have reached the point in this story where my character takes vengeance on the unsuspecting people of this sleepy beach town."

By day four, I was sitting next to Mike on the perfect white sofa sobbing, "What if I can't do this anymore? What if we can't be together?"

"We will always be together in a lot of ways," he said calmly. "We are best friends and parents together. I want you to be really happy, fully happy, whatever that means. You have my full support no matter what...I'm ready for whatever happens."

I believed him. I had decided I was ready too, whatever that would mean.

Soon after, we sat down with our two sons, who were then fourteen and fifteen years old. We told them that I'm gay, that we were friends, and that our relationship had changed over the years, but that we had always been honest with one another. We told them that we loved them very much and that would never change, and that we loved each other.

I watched their teenage faces quiet, still, absorbing. I didn't see any shock or anger, only what looked like compassion and a bit of relief. We were okay, they were thinking. Mike and I were holding hands and he was rubbing my back, trying to comfort me.

"Well, I'm really glad you told us," my youngest said first. "Really glad." He nodded at me looking extremely grown up.

"It's okay," said my oldest, "It's okay," he said again, looking directly at me. "But I do have some questions." He has always been very analytical and to the point. "So, Dad, are you gay as well?"

Mike laughed and quickly said, "No."

"So, this must be hard for you?" my son asked.

We all looked at Mike. "Yes and no," he said honestly. "We all need to support Mom right now and she needs to be able to live as herself."

I had been so terrified to share this news with the boys, not wanting to upset them, to disrupt their lives. I felt selfish for making this decision yet at the same time couldn't stand to be around them, knowing that I was keeping my true self from them.

The boys insisted that I immediately go and tell my parents to "keep the ball rolling," and offered to go with me. I declined their offer, but I did drive over to my parent's house that night and tell them. On the way, I felt calm and sure of what I was doing. My kids were right to encourage this and intuitively knew this was an important step for me. I felt calm all the way through the conversation with my parents, answering their questions as well as I could. They were both polite enough, although clearly afraid for me and the boys. They loved Mike like a son and had their own feelings of loss and grief to work through.

Each person I come out to brings with them a different set of expectations and emotions for me to manage. I am still often surprised that people have strong emotional reactions and opinions on how I should live my life. I've had to let go of people I never thought I'd lose—some days the pain and anger around that feels consuming. Then there are people who have held space for me in ways that I never thought I deserved, and I have been overwhelmed with gratitude. Either way, it is worth the price of admission to show up to this life fully and authentically as myself. I didn't realize at the time that keeping this part of myself separate from my kids and my community was not allowing me to live as myself, to live in alignment.

As difficult as it was, when I let go of relationships that couldn't support the true version of me, it made space for me to deepen many other relationships and brought new people into my life. This didn't happen immediately, but over time things began to shift. I knew that other people thought I was supposed to feel like I lost something, but I didn't. Instead, I felt closer to my kids; I felt honest around them. I had a clearer vision for my future that I was excited about.

I realized I wanted to be in a relationship that allowed me to be fully myself, and I wanted that for Mike as well. When I began planning to buy a house and the kids wanted it to be within walking distance of their dad, Mike and I worked together to make that happen.

Through all the awkward conversations, messy moments, and heartbreak, I felt excited for my future, excited to start showing up fully and authentically. If you are in the midst of this kind of change, know that as you persist on the path that is true for you, things will eventually improve. Being in alignment ultimately feels good.

The people we are surrounded by will act as mirrors to us. They help us feel where we are and are not living in alignment. When someone makes us angry or uncomfortable, these are opportunities to learn about ourselves. Likewise, when we crave the feeling of being around certain people, it is never just that person that is making us feel loved. Rather, it is that we are able to be our true selves around them.

When we are connected to our own love, our own essence, we live as our full self. It fills us with a sense of love and trust.

When I was a kid, I wanted to spend as much time with my grandmother as possible, and it was often at the beach. I would walk out on a jetty made of rocks in the middle of the ocean. I was a strong swimmer, and so was she, so she never seemed to mind how far I went. For me, to walk out on that jetty and not go to the end was pointless.

Towards the end of the jetty there was a part where the rocks had a large gap, and the only way to get across was to stretch my arms out to the next rock and jump at the same time. The bottom was slippery, so for one long moment I was completely in the air—before my hand gripped the rock and my feet landed. I wanted to get to the jetty's end because when I was closer to the water it felt as though I was completely submerged in the ocean. The best part of this experience was that I couldn't see or hear anything other than waves and sky. But I trusted the rocks that held me safe.

I often think of that jetty during major life changes or moments when we say to the Universe, "Yes, okay I will keep going. I know there is something for me on the other side I must experience." We're sometimes required to take this leap and for one moment we are suspended, not knowing exactly how we will land. In these groundless moments we can choose to give ourselves the grace and surrender to what will come. We can choose to leap and go forward without knowing the outcome; we can reach out our arms and ask the Universe to catch us, knowing we've done all we can do.

This knowing is also a practice. The first time I made that leap across the rocks was terrifying. Then I came to know that I would land safely. Over the years, my arms got longer, and it became second nature to do it.

One day after my rock climb as my grandmother was wrapping a towel around me, her neighbor marched over from the other side of the shore, still wearing her pajamas and looking angry. She stopped and stared at us for a second, seeming to question her decision to barge up to us. "That's not safe for her to do," she said accusingly. "She could slip right in."

My grandmother was a very loving woman with a gentle and calm demeanor; at home with me she had a very casual appearance, so people would often make the mistake of thinking they could say things like this to her. Once she spoke however, it was clear that her caring and calm came from a place of strength and knowing her worth. She had raised five boys, sat on government committees, and traveled the world—often by herself. One of her favorite sayings was that you catch more flies with honey than you do with vinegar. What I took that to mean was that she *chose* to be kind and polite. If people were not going where she was going, she asked them to please get out of her way.

So, she looked at her neighbor, let out a hum, and said, "She knows what she's doing," then put an arm around me and turned to walk back home.

She always had an awareness of how sensitive I was as a kid, and she must have known I felt strange about this woman watching me and then being critical of her. "That poor woman has a child who drowned," my grandmother said as we walked home. "So, she is always afraid when she watches you."

I thought about that and felt even more uncomfortable because it sounded like this woman was watching me all the time. My grandmother, sensing my discomfort, said, "There are always going to be people watching us do things that they are afraid of. It doesn't mean you can't climb on the rocks. Just smile, be polite, and do your thing."

Sometimes, as we begin to live in alignment, the people in our lives will have reactions to how we change. This usually comes from a place of fear. It is easy for people to stand on the shore and feel afraid watching something they believe is dangerous or wrong. They are afraid of what may happen to us, they are afraid of how the changes we make will affect those around us, and they are afraid of what it means for our relationship with them.

Cultivating your intuition and trusting it to set boundaries with people who are not ready to support you allows you to expend less energy trying to dissuade their fear. It's helps me to have people around who I can take advice and feedback from—the people who are also familiar with this leap of faith I choose to listen to, people who are putting themselves out there and living an authentic life. As much as we are going to love and have relationships with people who are—for whatever reason—standing on the shore watching in terror as we do something they don't agree with, we cannot live our lives in alignment with their fear. When people disagree with difficult decisions that affect my life, I try to take my grandmother's advice as much as possible: Be polite, smile, and do your thing, whatever that is.

EXERCISE: SETTING YOUR INTENTION DAILY PRACTICE

One of the first things I encourage clients to do is set intentions in their everyday lives. When it comes to developing your intuition, your intention is magic. The more you can believe in and give credibility to this magic in your life, the more it will become evident to you.

To create your reality, your intention is the most powerful thing you have. For all intents and purposes, it is a spell. In the beginning of intuitive development—as you are starting to examine and unlearn your conditioning—try to begin believing in yourself and this magic more and more. Words are an extension of your energy. Speaking out loud or writing down your intention sends a unique energetic vibration to the universe of what you desire and wish to accomplish.

To begin setting your intention at the beginning of the day:

- Find a quiet space where you won't be disturbed. Have something to write in—a journal or notebook. Sit with your eyes closed and just notice your breath for a few moments.

- With your thoughts, ask the Universe, your Guides, the Spirit World, or your own inner wisdom, "Where should I focus my intention for the day?" Focus on your breath until you feel, sense, know, see, or hear a response. Be open to receive this information in whatever form it comes to you.

- For example: if you are someone who feels deeply and when you sit you can feel the sunshine on your skin and have an overwhelming feeling of joy, perhaps your intention is to focus on finding joy and being outside. Or perhaps you hear a voice telling you to outline a creative project that you have been putting off, and suddenly you know exactly how simple this task will be.

- Write down the response you receive then look at and reflect for a moment on what you've written. Notice how your intention feels in your body. Start to notice the alignment taking shape within you.

- If, in these quiet moments with your morning intention you recognize that your inner knowing has the answer, you can begin to recognize it through your day.

5

My Story—On Birth & Death

"And I shall have some peace there, for peace comes dropping slow." – WB Yates

Sometimes I recommend that my clients meditate and "have a meeting" with their inner child or write a letter to their younger selves. This can be healing on many levels. Our older and wiser adult selves can often reconnect with the younger versions of us that still need assurance and healing.

As someone who's been in therapy for trauma, I have practiced this skill a lot. I've done this several times while writing this book—not so much to heal younger parts of myself, but to reassure myself that I am not that helpless child or teenager anymore. Someday, I imagine I will write a book about my near-death experience (NDE) from a healed place, and perhaps that will help someone with a similar experience heal or feel less alone. This is not that story, though.

I don't have a neat and tidy way to explain what happened to me or make sense of it. In fact, I actually have the opposite feeling: that my story is not yet complete. When I think about my NDE, I still feel very conflicted about it. When I feel uncomfortable with this, I try to surrender the need to understand, and instead trust that someday the understanding will come.

So far, my NDE has been presented to me in three parts, separated by near-perfect fourteen-year intervals—something that made me aware of the regenerative nature of the human body. While it cannot be said that we are completely new every fourteen years, it also cannot be said that we remain in the exact same body, which makes me wonder if our physical bodies are regenerating in alignment with our spiritual natures.

My three NDE experiences were: the premonition of it when I was almost eight years old; the experience itself when I was twenty-two; and the recap and clarity I had during trance work at thirty-six years old. Though I don't know why I have experienced these perfectly timed intervals, I write this from a place of curiosity, wonder, and an openness to have the answer when I am ready to receive it.

If I were going to write a letter to my twenty-two-year-old self naively stepping into a life-changing birth drama, it would go something like this:

> Dear Sheryl,
>
> I'm sorry that I haven't been there for you in the ways that you deserve. Those parts of you that you are most trying to hide are going to become the most cherished parts of yourself, but not for a long time. Things are about to break open in ways that you have not even imagined. Don't give up. After breaking open, there is going to be healing and love. So much love!
>
> Please stop blaming yourself for everything—it's going to be okay. The very scary news is that you are going to die soon and then you are going to come back and live, and neither of these things will be your choice. I'm thankful they are not your choice because otherwise, we may not be here. For as much pain as you are going to endure there will be an overwhelming sense of joy, love, and peace. Unfortunately, it's going to take a lot of time to get to the joy. Please hold on.
>
> You are going to realize that the inner you is powerful and that you can have everything you need to live this life. Though you are going to lose many people, don't be afraid to let them go.

You are going to meet amazing people who will love you for who you are—don't be afraid to stay open to that love.

You will read the last line of Mary Oliver's *The Summer Day* and you will smile as you answer, "I am going to live as myself." It will take time. Years from now you are going to cry and shout, "I have had enough! I am going to live in the light!" And by that point, you will have all the freedom and power you need to make every wish you've ever had come true.

Please hold on.

Surrender to it all.

It's good you are here.

PART ONE: A Premonition

When I was eight years old, we moved to a new home. It was a much larger house than we'd lived in before and we didn't have enough furniture for all the rooms. My favorite room was what I called "the piano room" because the only thing in it was our piano. One of my grandmother's friends had given it to me when I'd started taking lessons, but that was not the reason I was fond of the room. The truth was that it had white carpet and white walls with east-facing windows, so it flooded with morning sunlight, creating a perfect backdrop for the visions I was experiencing.

The visions were mostly in my mind's eye—energy dancing in rays of light and holographic-like images of animals and people on the blank walls. I would walk around the perimeter of the room, staying close to the walls for reasons I don't remember.

One day, I started to imagine a lady in front of me, coaxing me along. I told myself that I had "made her up," and that I was too old for imaginary friends. However, in my imagination (or perhaps my loneliness), I allowed myself to pretend with her. The more I allowed myself to see her, the more real she became. I had on my favorite outer space pajamas and couldn't imagine them being particularly interesting to anyone else, but then she said she liked my pajamas, and for a moment I had the feeling she might be real. I remember feeling a little uncomfortable about the compliment, and that was what made me feel she was so real. Why would I be imagining that?

I followed her around the room for what seemed like a long time until she said that I should lay down in the far corner. So, I did. I did not take naps as a kid, but suddenly, I felt *so* tired. When I closed my eyes, I felt a wave of exhaustion that seemed to pull me deep underwater, and I began to dream of being in a small white room. The lady was there, a man with a hat was there, and some other older people who all seemed familiar. I had a feeling of peace like everything was going to be okay. I remember feeling really comfortable in that dream like I didn't want to wake up.

When I felt my mother shaking me awake, I fought to keep my eyes closed; I wanted to stay in that room much more than I wanted to come back to my real life. My mom seemed very concerned since she had been looking for me and I hadn't answered her calls. It was unlike me to nap, so she decided I must be sick and needed to stay in bed for the rest of the day.

I didn't think much about this dream again, but from time to time I would notice the lady—and sometimes the man with the hat—appear out of the corner of my eye, in my imagination, or in my dreams.

I felt they were watching me, especially when things were difficult (like when I had to speak in school).

When I was thirteen, I saw them clearly again. I had run away from home in the middle of the night, tying a bedsheet together and climbing out my second-story window like Anne of Green Gables. The man and woman were there, simply watching me without judgment. I didn't realize at this time that the lady, the man with the hat, and the white room would become a significant part of my life and NDE years later.

PART TWO: Birth and Death

In 2004 I was pregnant with my first son and had a relatively easy pregnancy until the last two weeks when my blood pressure slowly started to climb. Up until that point, I had been able to work part-time selling cars and part-time in the marketing department, so I didn't have to run around quite as much. I took prenatal yoga classes at the local hospital but hadn't given much thought to what it would be like to give birth, or even to be a mother. I read a lot about what was happening to my body in pregnancy, which I found fascinating.

But I read nothing about what happens when you give birth, or what to do after you have a baby. I was not prepared for even a normal birth experience—never mind the horror I was about to go through. I never thought it possible that I wouldn't bring my baby home to his freshly painted nursery until he was three months. And I had certainly not considered the possibility of wanting to die—or of actually dying. In the days before my son was born, twenty-two-year-old me naively drove around singing "Happy Birthday," thinking that might entice him to arrive on time. I was a little nervous about breastfeeding but hadn't imagined I'd need to pump my breast milk and throw it away because of the high amounts of morphine in it—morphine I would later have to fight to get off of.

I'd never heard of women having seizures while giving birth and I'd certainly never heard of the rare HELPS syndrome—a horrid condition that would cause my organs to shut down as doctors frantically tried to deliver a baby who had a cord wrapped around his neck. I'd never considered asking my family to donate blood so I could have a transfusion after almost bleeding to death. I just drove around, sipping on coffee ice cream sodas and singing "Happy Birthday," convinced that everything was going to be fine.

In retrospect, I had a blank spot about how motherhood would be and couldn't imagine it at all. I had no images of snuggling a baby or sitting in the nursery rocking my new son...just a blank space. I couldn't foresee that three days after the birth—after I was transferred to a larger hospital with a NICU—I'd call my best friend who answered the phone with an excited, "Sheryl!" and simply say, "It didn't go well."

This has been a recurring theme throughout my life. When I simply can't picture an impending event, it's likely not going to happen. In this case, it didn't happen in a way that I could process.

During my birth drama, the chaos did not slow down. Doctors and nurses kept hurrying in and out of the operating room. All I could feel was pain and intense nausea. I focused my attention on the most troubling—the pain in my arms which were strapped to the table for some reason and shaking uncontrollably. For one moment I imagined how good it would feel to have them wrapped around me and for the painful tremors to stop, then the next moment would pull my attention back to the nausea.

I thought the birth must nearly be over because I could hear my son crying, which meant he was okay. Everyone seemed relieved, and Mike went to hold the baby.

"Look," someone said, clearly expecting me to turn my head to look at my son. I felt shocked that anyone would ask this of me. Didn't they realize how impossible it was for me to move? Wanting to see, yet not having the energy to speak, I used all my strength to rotate my head from right to left. But a fresh wave of nausea rolled through me, my teeth chattered, and I tasted blood on my lips from biting down on them. I finally finished turning my head and managed to look in the direction of my son. There he was, eight feet away from me. I knew Mike was holding him, but I could only see a bleary, bright mass of swaddled softness that felt out of place in this horror story.

Then, all of a sudden, I had an audible thought and heard my own voice say, "I want to die now."

I felt my eyes close, and slowly, sweetly, felt pulled beneath the surface of the agony of my body—it was euphoric. I somehow began to move up above myself to the ceiling and looked down at the pieces of my human form. Two people were working to put everything back together, but thankfully, I couldn't feel any of this now. It was the most serene feeling of escape, like waking up early for school on a weekend and realizing you could go back to sleep.

The image of my old body faded, and I woke up. Or, I thought I did.

I opened my eyes and was in a white room similar to the room from my premonition at eight years old, except it felt smaller. The feeling of serenity continued as I looked around a room that could have made me feel claustrophobic, but instead made me feel safe and held. There were familiar faces—the man with the hat and the lady from the piano room. My great-grandmother Florence was also there. She had always been a little frightening to me when I was a child because she had Alzheimer's, but now she seemed sweet and kind and lucid.

The next thing I remember is waking up and screaming in pain.

At least I thought I was screaming, but it turns out that scream was only in my mind. "Help," I whispered louder and louder until someone came into the room. "Help me," I said over and over as nurses continued to run around, eventually connecting a morphine drip that did not help.

It was twelve hours before I could fully speak again. "Where is my baby?" I whispered harshly to a young nurse who had come to check my blood pressure and now looked very startled by my tone.

She scurried out of the room without speaking and a different nurse appeared with my son a few minutes later, cheerful, and congratulatory. She seemed confused and concerned by the ominous mood of the room and as she carefully tried to pass my son to me it became clear I was not strong enough for this task. She glanced left to right where my mom and sister were keeping watch over me, silently pleading for them to help. My mom jumped to her feet, expertly taking the baby from her. Leaning on the side of the bed for leverage so as not to put any pressure on my body, she positioned my son in a way that made it seem like I was holding him.

We were facing each other now, and as I looked into his eyes, I felt like we'd known each other for a lifetime. "I know you," I said.

Now everything around why I never could picture this when I was pregnant made sense. I had no reference point for this type of experience. That I could die, come back to life, and be holding my baby all within a twelve-hour period was absolutely beyond my imagination.

I wish I could say that I was fine from that point on, but the nightmare continued for another few months. Through the many hospital visits and two more surgeries, none got me close to that euphoric feeling of death I now found myself craving. Every time I opened my eyes, I was disappointed to be back in my body again.

And I couldn't express this feeling because of my overwhelming guilt at wanting to leave this earth when clearly, I was needed. What kind of mother looks at her baby and thinks, "I want to die?"

Of all the secrets I'd been carrying as I suffered to process my experiences and flashbacks, the worst part— as I confessed to my therapist ten years later—was the guilt of wanting to die in the moments and days after becoming a mother. I still wanted to live but visiting the Spirit World had given me such a feeling of euphoria and belonging, nothing in my physical world could compare to it.

"I don't see it that way at all," my therapist said carefully. "The way I see it, your body was dying. Your organs were failing, and you'd suffered major blood loss and seizures. When our body is dying, we know; it's instinctual. At some point we accept it. The way I see it, is that you knew your son was okay; you had made it through this whole experience and held on."

When I said I didn't understand, she explained, "I'm saying that you didn't see your baby and want to die. You saw that he was okay, and you knew that it was finally safe to let go."

Oh, I thought, maybe that's true.

"You could feel proud of yourself that you made it that far and held on to make sure he was okay."

There it was: the breakthrough I'd needed. It was so simple yet so complex to unpack the way I thought about myself in the worst light. Why had I assumed that I was such a horrible person? Why had that been the easiest thought? Throughout everything I'd gone through, I'd made myself the villain of the story. I couldn't even give myself compassion as I was dying.

The truth was, it had been easier to believe I'd wanted to die, and now it was scarier to know that it was beyond my control.

PART THREE: Putting the Pieces Together

In 2018, when I was thirty-six, I was lucky enough to make it back to study at The Arthur Findlay College for the second time. In what was one of my most revealing weeks of self-discovery, I was lucky to study with renowned spiritual medium and tutor, Eamonn Downey.

On day three on our class, I was seated on the platform with several other mediums for a small trance demonstration. Trance mediumship is perhaps one of the most misunderstood aspects of mediumship —what is often seen in movies and pop culture as something scary and strange is actually very simple. Trance is an altered state where the medium blends with the Spirit World, becoming unaware of their body and mind, and invites Spirit into their personal space. When we are in trance, we are not taken over or possessed by the Spirit World. Instead, we are surrounded by Spirit and being held very closely. To make space for the Spirit World to be with us, we need to trust this process and be secure in surrendering to it. To achieve a true state of trance, we need to practice moving the conscious mind aside so it will not interfere with this process.

I had been practicing trance for some time and it not only felt natural to me, but it also held an element of the euphoric feeling I experienced in my near-death experience.

I focused on my breathing as my conscious mind moved further away while the Spirit World moved closer. As I focused, I began to see an ocean. It was dark; I was swimming at night and rocking with the waves. Suddenly I was being tossed back and forth and pulled underwater. Then suddenly everything changed, and I was in the white room. My guides were there, just watching me. I felt the rise and fall of my breathing in a way that frightened me—like someone was breathing for me. I clearly saw my eight-year-old self experiencing the premonition. I then saw my near-death experience and how it had unfolded, but this time from a perspective that was not mine. The sensation of not breathing on my own was still with me. I stayed suspended in that space for what felt like only a minute or two, but in real time, was nearly thirty minutes.

When I came back into the room and opened my eyes, the class was staring at me. My teacher asked what I had experienced and not having the words to describe it, I said truthfully, "I'm not sure."

"I'll give you some more time to think about it," he said. "Because that was like Christmas and Thanksgiving and New Year's all rolled into one, so you must have some idea what happened."

"My guides were showing me an experience," I said after a few moments, "something that happened to me where I couldn't breathe. They were showing how they were with me." I started to get choked up and said, "Then they showed me another time when I was young and when I had a premonition of that experience."

The teacher nodded very kindly and said, "Yes that's right. You were never alone there. I hope you can see that now."

I am very grateful for that experience and to have had a teacher who knew to push me to speak about what had happened, to give me the opportunity to process it as well as to remember.

Sometimes trance experiences can be like a dream—if we don't make an instant record of it, we can lose the memory of it forever.

This is the part of the story where I feel I fall short by not having some tidy and profound way to tie everything neatly together for you. My feelings are anything but tidy—instead, they are conflicted and messy. I'm not sure why this happened to me and I'm not sure what it means. I feel angry it happened and at the same time I am grateful. I enjoy having the memory of dying and I loathe the memory of returning to life.

The NDE made me unafraid of death. Though it has given me permission to live more fully without fear, at the same time PTSD from the experience kept me trapped inside myself for years. Ultimately, I've decided that it is okay not to understand at this moment.

I have a sign hanging in my living room that says, "It's good you are here." I make myself read it every day, even though sometimes I want to roll my eyes because it's not like I have a choice in the matter. At the same time as believing the sign's message, I acknowledge that I've had to fight really hard to be here.

On occasion, if a grieving client asks me what it feels like to die, I will describe my experience to them. To be able to provide a sense of peace to someone else when they are afraid for their loved ones is perhaps the greatest NDE gift of all. Conversely, at the same time, I am conflicted—angry even—at having to describe it. Either way, no matter where I am on either side of life, I believe the sign. I tell myself "It's good you are here," and choose to surrender to that belief.

Coming Back to Life: Intuition and Healing

The years I spent in survival mode with unprocessed trauma are not easy to recall. Often, I find I have just enough memories to piece my story together. The things I did to cope during that period left me feeling disconnected from my body, which then left me disconnected from my intuition and mediumship abilities. My eating disorder, denial of my sexuality, and refusal to feel emotions were my way of refusing to engage in living. That refusal greatly limited my ability to connect to myself, receive intuitive messages, and understand them.

Whenever I had a NDE flashback, I could feel a panic attack coming on. I would see myself from above, almost like I was looking at myself from across the room or from the ceiling. My mind protected me by disconnecting from my body, but it was a challenge when it came to processing emotions from a healthy place.

For years, I would wake up on my son's birthday feeling exactly like I had waking up in the hospital all those years ago: I could smell the iodine; I could hear machines beeping. I felt afraid yet also unemotional and disconnected.

Strangely, the same feeling of love and gratitude for the people who were taking care of me back then also returned. I felt deeply grateful to my mom for all she did to care for me in the months after my experience. It was the closest I had ever felt to her, and every year around the anniversary of my trauma, my gratitude was like a thread that pulled us closer—I reexperienced her protecting me and physically caring for me.

Besides this consistently difficult anniversary, any time I felt my son was threatened, it would retrigger my trauma. Whenever that happened, I often walked between two worlds—living in the present emotional devastation at my child being mistreated and living in the past, experiencing the terror of losing him.

The passage of time has also been really important in processing everything. For highly sensitive and intuitive people I can't say this enough: give yourself lots of time. It has taken fifteen years for me to be able to put my experience into words, and it is still a struggle. Just know that gratitude is never helpful when it is forced upon us. Only for the last five years of my long process did I have the idea of gratitude and was aware that I *wanted* to feel grateful for my experience.

Yet I am still conflicted by anger and grief. It is very common for trauma to compound, and I feel that my lack of memories is a result of this. Consequently, I've had to work backwards to uncover my feelings. Never having processed the trauma of being sexually assaulted, being in an abusive relationship, my friend dying, and then my own near-death experience was just too much to look at all at once.

To make peace, I had to slowly unravel these early years. For a long time, the idea that everything happened far in the past really stopped me from engaging in the healing processes I needed. For anyone dealing with compounded trauma, know that timelines are not important. I wish I would have given myself permission earlier to feel the grief and pain that I needed to, instead of shaming myself into repressing it.

Navigating my PTSD was one of the most difficult things I've ever had to do. I felt like I was fighting my way back from the past with everything I had. My vivid imagination played both negative and positive roles in my PTSD recovery, and I found there is a close connection between PTSD and ADHD. Once I was able to accurately diagnose and treat my ADHD, it significantly helped with my PTSD flashbacks and intrusive thoughts. Many people who experience clairvoyance have very active imaginations— often thinking in pictures instead of words. I believe this contributed to the depth of accuracy in which my mind would recreate my traumatic experiences. I also know that this helped in my recovery.

During my second pregnancy, I began practicing meditation and visualization, which I think were especially helpful because I could use my vivid imagination to enhance those events. Many people wonder why, if I had such a traumatic experience with my first son—especially with a twenty percent risk of my condition reoccurring—did I have another baby only twenty months later. I recognize this pattern in earlier trauma as well. After I was sexually assaulted as a teenager, I frequently put myself in unsafe situations.

Through years of therapy, I've learned that I needed to recreate these experiences to correct the trauma. When I got pregnant again, a subconscious part of me felt that having another baby where I could control or create a positive experience would help me heal.

When I went for my first prenatal appointment, I expected to see my doctor, had a lot of questions surrounding the birth experience, and wanted to be prepared. It was when I discovered that I wouldn't be seeing her at this appointment that I had my first panic attack. The nurses in the office knew my history and were quick to react—they immediately got me to the office of a gifted therapist, Dianna, who was key in my recovery and survival those first few years.

She began a visual meditation right away to help me calm down, then introduced me to meditation and the idea that I could alter my mental state through visualizations and breathwork. I began seeing her twice a week during my pregnancy. Some weeks I would go into her office and in my meditative state wouldn't even remember the hour. Developing this skill was one of the most helpful tools in the early part of my recovery. I was able to make a birth plan for my second son and it was a deeply healing experience.

One of the most challenging aspects of those early healing years was feeling invalidated by the reactions of other people. As a culture, we tend to place all our interests on "the baby" in the birth experience—the mother is often seen (even expected to be) as selfless, giving, and self-sacrificing. The ways in which other people wanted to frame my story to make it more comfortable for them made me angry: a selfless mother; brave for having a second child; you both nearly died; you must have mixed emotions about his birthday; over-protective. All of these were infuriating and unhelpful to hear.

Recovering from a near-death experience and being physically and mentally devastated while being expected to be selfless and serene felt dehumanizing. People I thought loved me came to visit and doted on my baby then—as an afterthought—joked, "Oh, and nice to see you too Sheryl!". Working through my rage at visitors who came to see me and took my baby from my arms without any regard for my well-being was a big part of my recovery work.

My ex-husband Mike was one of the few people who validated my experience, telling everyone that, "It was the worst thing I've ever seen. Worse than anything I'd seen in combat." I was grateful to have him as a witness to my experience.

Doctors and therapists also named my experience, and eventually I was able to name that near-death experience for myself—it was a validating and crucial part of my healing. Only after a lot of healing did I realize that I wanted to tell my story.

I began to attract people who would tell me about their own near-death experiences. At first, these stories seemed ridiculous to me. There was a woman who told me she'd had a near-death experience after receiving anesthesia during knee surgery, and there have been several mediums who've told me that they were "taken to the Spirit World in a near-death experience."

While I quietly listened to these recounts, in my head I was screaming. It was offensive that people wanted to have the near-death experience label without any of the death.

Finally, a friend used the title near-death experience to describe a deep meditation they'd experienced from the comfort of their own home, and I was forced to reconcile these feelings. That same weekend, I attended a mediumship seminar where the teacher matter-of-factly shared with me after class about her own NDE after a car accident. Unlike some of the aggravating encounters I'd had, when she shared this, I recognized the familiarity in our energy and knew that she had also been to the Spirit World. I don't know how else to explain it, other than to say sometimes our soul will recognize a commonality with others—just like psychic people, empaths, and mediums have a way of recognizing each other.

I felt safe sharing my feelings of anger and resentment with her. She listened kindly and when she spoke, I felt as though she had seen my experience through the same soul recognition I'd had. She didn't ask me any questions or try to rewrite my narrative for me, she simply said "When you are ready, you're going to tell this story your way, and that will heal some of this. You know what death feels like and so do I, so we don't have a need to explain it to everyone, we just know."

I felt my experience was truly understood by her and it gave me a sense of peace. I also believed her that I would tell this story in my own way and began to imagine that as a significant part of my life. My anger at people calling their spiritual experiences NDEs was really useful to figuring out my own life path. Emotions— anger in particular—often lead us in the right direction and uncover what is not healed within us.

I'm in no way saying I am an authority on the experiences of others; everyone should use language they feel comfortable with. Medically speaking, a NDE is when our body is close to death or on the brink of death and we have a spiritual experience. I freely admit that out-of-body experiences where someone feels they are experiencing the Spirit World but without being near-death (yet described as NDE's) are still difficult for me relate to because I still can't understand using that terminology without experiencing the near-death part.

It feels dismissive to me.

I believe this is more evidence of not being fully healed from my experience. Perhaps this short telling of my story will help that process.

Being able to discuss the experience with my son has also been a part of my healing. He'd heard bits and pieces before, but never my feelings about what had happened to us both. Never wanting to take away from his birthday celebrations or project my feelings of grief onto his special day, I had never shared how difficult that time of year had always been for me.

A few years ago, we were hiking through the woods, and I decided to share the details with him. He listened to me talk about the PTSD and my nightmares. I shared some of my anger and feelings about death, how I was still angry, and how I had started to feel grateful for the experience because it had taught me so much about the Spirit World. He listened quietly and then surprised me by saying, "So my birthday must be really hard for you. It must be hard to make a cake every year and pretend you are happy. I mean, I know you are happy I was born, but that must also have been the worst day of your life."

"It has been very hard," I answered honestly. "And I guess it was the worst day of my life that also ended up bringing one of the best people I know into the world. It's not just one or the other, it is both."

2

Part Two

Exploring Your Intuition

6

Receiving Intuitive Information

Exploring The Clairs

Everyone is intuitive and receives information every day through their physical senses. Seeing, hearing, smelling, feeling, and tasting help you experience the world. Your intuition, although often referred to as a "sixth sense," will use your physical senses to communicate to you—most commonly through seeing, hearing, feeling, and knowing. These intuitive senses are sometimes called "The Clairs": clairvoyance, clairaudience, clairsentience, and claircognizance are most commonly experienced by highly sensitive and intuitive people.

Recognizing how you receive information intuitively will help you strengthen your abilities, and once you know how you receive information most easily, you can begin to develop your abilities. The impressions we receive always have a feeling; recognizing that feeling benefits us as we build confidence in our abilities. At some point, most people will use all these senses to receive information, although one sense is often stronger than another. That said, all humans are naturally clairsentient and able to feel information, so if you are not sure which sense is strongest for you, start by developing your clairsentience.

Clairsentience

Clairsentience (or "clear feeling") may be the most valuable yet undervalued way we receive information. Because we are often taught to dismiss our feelings, many intuitive people discredit and question the strong clairsentient messages they receive—but we feel that information all the same.

Remember a time when you walked into a room where an argument had just occurred, and you could feel that energy? Remember the last time you had a "gut feeling"? That is clairsentience. But it is often more than just a generalized gut feeling. Through clairsentience, you can receive detailed impressions and messages.

Highly clairsentient people may:

- feel strongly affected by the emotions of others
- feel a strong connection to animals and plants
- find that people, even strangers, easily confide in them
- spend a lot of time helping others

Clairvoyance

Clairvoyance means "clear seeing." In psychic and mediumship work the word is often used to describe the ability to "see" the Spirit World, images they present, and psychic visions. Some people will also refer to themselves as "a clairvoyant," meaning that they can see this way.

There are two types of clairvoyance: subjective and objective.

Subjective Clairvoyance is the most common and refers to images and visions that appear in the same space as your imagination—in your mind's eye. It's sometimes called "intuitive clairvoyance". Have you ever met someone and begun to see images of their life? Maybe you can easily imagine what their home looks like or who they spend time with, almost like watching a movie? Perhaps they are dressed in a suit and tie, but you can easily imagine them coaching a kids baseball game. This movie inside your mind may be your clairvoyance. It's common to experience clairvoyance yet dismiss it as imagination. One way to tell the difference is that with clairvoyance, images may appear in just a flash, however, you will be able to recall them clearly and easily.

Objective Clairvoyance refers to seeing images outside your mind; they may appear holographic, like seeing a spirit person sitting in your living room.

Objective clairvoyance was how I connected to the Spirit World most naturally as a child. I knew there was something "wrong" with my eyes—that it was never dark when I closed them. I knew I was sensitive to light, especially when I began having migraines at the age of eight. Even then, I was at peace with this difference and not alarmed or surprised when I would objectively "see" things.

When I began "seeing a lot behind my eyes" with my eyes closed, I was both distracted and fascinated. I would look at printed wallpapers or daydream in class and images would appear—sometimes in patterns on the wallpaper, sometimes in a cloud of dust when rays of the sun shone through the window. It could be anywhere.

My visions were usually very subtle—I find this important to explain to clients at the beginning of their intuition development journey. Clairvoyance is often subtle. It takes great sensitivity to perceive energy so strongly that our mind interprets this vibration as an image. If we are waiting for spirit people to appear to us as they would in a Hollywood movie, we are waiting for the wrong thing. In mediumship and psychic work, we learn to live in that subtle world of energy that is always available to us as intuitive people.

When my great-grandmother was alive, she talked about seeing spirit people. A cousin of hers who had passed would visit her at night and they would have "chats" as he sat at the end of her bed. After a while, though, the visits started to frighten her and one night she told him not to come to visit again. He never returned. By the time I heard this story as a child, I had interpreted it to mean that she was right to be afraid—not of the spirit person but of what might happen to her if she had decided to share this information.

My grandmother was hospitalized for being "hysterical" in the 1970s. Still grieving the loss of her young child to leukemia, she gave birth to her eighth child, a girl, who was stillborn. She began having panic attacks and committed herself to a psychiatric hospital.

These stories of seeing ghosts and being trapped because of hysteria shaped my (un)willingness to discuss the things I saw. That, and the strong desire of everyone around me not to speak of such things.

Many clairvoyant people:

- think in pictures rather than words
- remember faces better than names
- have vivid imaginations
- enjoy art, nature, or interior design
- resonate with symbols and colors
- are visual learners
- have vivid dreams or visions

Clairaudience

Clairaudience is when someone "hears" information from the Spirit World. It is not our physical ears that hear, rather it's our mind interpreting energy as a sound. You may have even experienced clairaudience without realizing it. While developing this ability, you may expect to hear a different voice in your mind and sometimes it's the voice of someone you recognize. But most often it will be your own voice. Common ways people experience clairaudience are hearing their name called softly from another room, song lyrics that suddenly come into your mind, or hearing random words inside your mind spoken in your own voice.

Many clairaudient people:

- easily recall names and dates
- hear buzzing or ringing in their ears
- are sensitive to sounds
- enjoy reading and writing
- easily remember the lyrics to songs
- call easily recall the quality of someone's voice
- prefer auditory learning

It's important to note the connection between "hearing voices" and mental health. Over the last few years, I've encountered several clients developing their mediumship who have shared with me that the Spirit World "told them to do something," and my response is always the same: The Spirit World does not command things from us or give us specific directions. Instead, they impart a sense of unconditional love and support. The Spirit World will never play tricks on you, cause you harm, or tell you to harm yourself or another person. They are not punitive in nature, they do not provide consequences for our actions, nor do they withhold communication or love from us.

If you ever hear voices that encourage you to harm yourself or others, please seek professional mental health help. There is no shame in asking for help, and you do not need to navigate those experiences alone.

Claircognizance

When you are experiencing Claircognizance, it feels like "just knowing" something without knowing how you know. The information is simply in your mind—you may even feel like you are making it up. Trusting this strong feeling of knowing is one of the most powerful ways to communicate with your intuition.

Many claircognizant people:

- feel like information is being downloaded to them
- enjoy deep discussions about spiritual topics
- desire to study and understand the meaning of things
- seem to easily make snap decisions
- have a lot of ideas
- enjoy solving problems

Psychometry: Learning from Objects

In addition to the Clairs, psychometry gives us another way of knowing. The word derives from the Greek word "psyche" meaning soul and "metro" meaning to measure and refers to the psychic ability to read or sense energy from an object.

The term was coined by Professor of Physiology Joseph Buchanan, who experimented with his students by having them "read" objects. He published his findings in his book *Journal of Man* (Buchanan 1887), theorizing that objects have souls that retain a memory. In the same vein, Michael Talbot's book *The Holographic Universe* (Talbot 1991) suggests that "the past is not lost, but still exists in some form accessible to human perception." He asserts that consciousness and reality exist in a kind of hologram that contains a record of the past, present, and future, and that people with psychometric abilities may be able to tap into that record.

While I love to study and understand how energy works, I also recognize that there is no need to define or prove how psychometry works because I know from experience that it does. Energy can never be lost or destroyed, and so every object or place will have an energetic "footprint." As a psychic or highly intuitive person holding or seeing an object, you can sense and feel that energy.

Though much of the research on psychometry revolves around holding an object, I no longer believe it's necessary to physically touch an object to read its energy. Much in the same way that we can access the energy of a place or person from a photograph, people with psychic ability can simply look at an object.

In my work, I coach developing mediums and intuitive students from all over the world through virtual sessions. By simply seeing an object or photograph virtually, nearly all of my students have been able to easily read energy or "tune in " to a person or place, in much the same way I am able to conduct mediumship readings in Boston with someone who is in Australia, the UK, or Hawaii.

Very often when I am working with mediumship students in a psychometry exercise, I will feel the energy shift as a spirit person will come in to work with them. Students will go from explaining details of the object's past to affirmative statements of, "Now she is showing me where she used to live..." Psychometry seems to be a really powerful way many people connect both intuitively and "mediumistically" if working with a Spirit Person.

Trust Yourself: You Know More Than You Think You Do

As you explore your intuitive abilities, try not to get caught up in wishing one of your senses was stronger, or that you could receive information differently or like someone else. A lot of people put significance on clairvoyance because they have been conditioned to think that "seeing is believing." Now that I have begun to understand my clairvoyance and work as a medium, I know that "seeing" is not my strongest sense—feeling and knowing are how the Spirit World and my intuition communicate the easiest.

If you imagine having a conversation using only one sense, you might think that it would be far easier to just "know and feel" information rather than trying to play charades and interpret messages and information from images alone, yet this is different for everyone and depends on how much they see. For example, in the beginning of understanding my mediumship, I struggled with seeing lots of Spirit People. Because I could never be quite sure if I was "seeing" the person I was communicating with or another Spirit Person connected to them, I quickly figured out that I needed to wait to give a physical description to my recipient. Sometimes I would clairvoyantly see a living person in their life as well! It was all very confusing in the beginning because it's one thing to have our own relationship with the Spirit World and communicate with them, and quite another to relay messages and explain the process to clients.

This is why—no matter how strong our connection may be—intuitive development takes time, practice, and trust in ourselves and the process.

As you begin to regularly develop your intuition, pay extra attention to the difference between your mind assigning meaning to something or your intuition communicating with you. You may have heard that with intuition, the first thing that comes to mind is usually the answer. This can be true because the mind has not yet had a chance to form an impression or interfere.

The job of your conscious mind has been to keep you safe your entire life. Your mind wants you to be comfortable and safe and will always choose the path of least resistance to avoid discomfort, pain, or embarrassment, which is why starting or stopping a habit can be so challenging. Since you've likely had a lifetime of letting your conscious mind control your behavior and decision making, it will take time and may be an uncomfortable challenge to learn to trust this new way of operating from intuition. Be patient with yourself as you practice.

When you begin practicing, there is an important distinction between tuning in and the need to find the "right" answer. Forming an open-ended question rather than one with a yes-or-no answer will allow you to determine when you are receiving information rather than reaching for a specific answer from your own mind.

For example, if someone asks me during a mediumship reading, "How many children did she have?" my conscious mind will want to interject, to guess the right answer. My mind will wonder, "Is it two children or three?" and it may become hard to know where the information is coming from. A better way to answer this question is for me to "tune in" or become curious about children. I may start to see them one by one or feel into the personality of the children I see. I may see a table with a family sitting around it and focus on simply noticing who is there, which allows me to feel the mood, personalities, and conversations happening. By being open, I allow my intuition to guide me rather than my conscious mind.

Try not to assign meaning with your mind, but rather tune in using your intuition. Maintaining an attitude of curiosity rather than a need to explain and "get it right" will be most supportive as you develop your abilities.

Breath: A Bridge to Your Intuition

I first began meditating to relieve anxiety and PTSD symptoms after the birth of my first child. My therapist taught that practicing breathwork and meditation could bring the same results as medication to lower my blood pressure and slow trauma responses. During my mediumship training in the UK, I learned that this breathwork would also be an important part of my mediumship and intuitive work.

Bringing awareness to breathing helps you tap into your true essence and connect to your own spirit—the basis for intuitive work. Breathing helps circulate energy in our bodies as well as relax us. Many eastern practices like yoga and tai chi use breathwork to tune into our bodies, develop self-awareness, and feel deeper emotions.

Your breath is an anchor for meditation, intuitive work, and mediumship. As you begin to connect with your intuition, your conscious mind will always want to interfere, because most of us have many thoughts coming in and out of our mind at any given moment. Focusing on your breath will occupy the conscious mind and allow you to receive information through your intuitive senses more easily.

One of the first books I read on mediumship was *A Guide for the Development of Mediumship* by Harry Edwards. Published in 1956 before the rise in popularity of breathwork in the West, Edwards talks about the importance of "entering into the stillness" and introduces The Mirror of the Mind concept in which he states, "The consciousness is unable to hold two distinct sets of thought impressions at the same time. Hence, the developing medium has the need to learn the way of clearing the mirror of physical thought and so allow it to receive spirit thought and impressions" *(A Guide for the Development of Mediumship Edwards 1956).* Focusing on the breath is the most simple and effective way to "clear our mind."

As you begin to decode and understand your intuitive abilities, I encourage you to keep a journal, a record of clairvoyance images, experiences, and journaling after meditation practices. It will become a future gift you give yourself. Simply noting a few sentences about what's happening in your development, what you are working on, and where you'd like to be in the future can powerfully embed them as a part of your new reality and increase your understanding your experiences.

EXERCISE 1: VISUALIZATION & MINDFULNESS

Visualization and mindfulness exercises strengthen your clairvoyance. They help you recognize images, hold images for longer, and understand the difference between images from your mind vs. images from your intuition.

Begin with this simple visualization & mindfulness exercise:

Go for a walk outside and notice the small details of your surroundings. Pay attention to every blade of grass, every cloud in the sky, the texture of the ground. Pay attention to the colors you see, the various shades and depth of them. Rather than trying to look for something interesting or extraordinary, allow yourself to simply notice the detail of what is. Notice how each leaf is different, how the clouds have varying shapes, and how the light reflects uniquely to create shadows around everything it touches.

Whenever you have a moment later that day, close your eyes and use your imagination to bring up the images you focused on during your walk. As you recall a leaf, flower, or rock, notice how long you can hold that image in your mind without it changing. In the beginning, most likely it will only be for a second or two, but this can be developed with practice until you will be able to hold the images for a longer and longer amount of time.

This practice develops a sense of mindfulness and connects you to your surroundings—both of which are helpful in developing your intuition. By staying present, you allow yourself to connect to your inner wisdom. Intuition happens in the moment, not when we are worrying about the future or lamenting about the past.

EXERCISE 2: VISUAL "DAYDREAMS"

Find a place in your home to sit quietly. Take a few deep breaths. This allows your body to relax as well as gives your conscious mind something to focus on so that it can stay out of the way. Choose a question or situation, preferably one where you are not deeply attached to the outcome. Then sit and focus on your breath, beginning to let your eyes relax, your vision soften, and allow yourself to go off into a soft daydream stare. Gazing at a blank wall or a patterned surface that is not significant to you will help keep your conscious mind from intervening.

Here are a few examples of open-ended and not highly emotional topics:

- What do I need to know about this upcoming meeting?
- What is something in nature that I will notice when I am connecting to my intuition?
- What do I need to know about this upcoming situation or event?
- Who will I speak to in the next few days that I am not expecting?
- What will bring me unexpected joy in the near future?
- What do I need to know to make this decision?

After a few moments, you may start to notice images appearing on the space where you are focusing. Write these images down. After a few moments of simply allowing yourself to be and notice and record, go back to each image and examine them with curiosity. Write down your impressions. Try not to assign meaning with your mind but use your intuition instead. And don't be afraid to use Google or a dream dictionary if your intuition leads you in that direction. Maintaining an attitude of curiosity rather than a need to explain and "get it right" will be your most supportive mindset.

I did this exercise when I was booking my trip to Arthur Findlay college in the UK. Sitting in my office and staring at the patterned wallpaper I asked, "What do I need to know about making the decision to take this trip?" Immediately, two images appeared on the wall— a giraffe and a skeleton. The giraffe I immediately took to mean seeing off in the distance, seeing for miles and miles. This was a symbol I often had in dreams and associated with uniqueness, happiness, and long-term goals. Great, I thought, that makes sense.

However, I didn't have an easy meaning for the skeleton, and of course my mind quickly interjected, "You're going to die." Images of a fiery plane crash went well with the skull and bones I had seen on my wall. Nevertheless, I quickly dismissed this because I had a strong, positive feeling about the skeleton and a longstanding fear of flying. After all, I was excited about my trip, I booked the last available spot on the course, and had the full support of my family. I knew in my heart that this was where I was meant to go. I went to my dream dictionary to look up the meaning of skeletons to see if it resonated. The first definition, "a secret or skeleton in your closet" didn't resonate, so I dismissed it. The next one made more sense: "Something that is not fully developed, in the planning stages, transformation."

That made sense to me.

7

Signs & Synchronicities

Proof: Signs from The Spirit World

During my first year of practicing mediumship professionally, I did a mediumship reading for a young woman who had lost her husband a few years earlier. He had a wonderful sense of humor and presented me with lots of evidence. In a mediumship reading, spirit people will present evidence to the medium of their personalities, hobbies, memories, etc. that will be recognizable to their loved ones, so those loved ones know that the spirit person continues to be with them after they have passed to the Spirit World. The reading was going well, and we both felt his presence strongly.

"This is strange," I said to her. "I keep seeing a raccoon. Does that mean something to you?"

"No," she said, looking confused.

"Okay," I replied and continued on to something else.

Her husband showed me their last vacation, a special memory, and something their son had recently accomplished. The father was so proud of him. Then there was that raccoon again, and I ignored it. As I continued reading, I started to hear The Beatles song "Rocky Raccoon" playing loudly in my mind.

I looked at the woman across from me, "There must be something with a raccoon. What about this song "Rocky Raccoon"? Do you understand this from your husband?"

"I really can't think of anything," she said.

"Rocky Raccoon..." the lyrics continued playing loudly in my head. Again, I moved on and shortly after finished the reading.

When the woman was leaving my office, she thanked me, and we hugged.

"Keep an eye out for that raccoon!" I said, the words popping out of my mouth almost involuntarily.

She gave me a kind-but-skeptical look, smiled, and thanked me again.

After the reading, I sat in my chair and asked the husband what that was all about.

"You'll see," he said.

It would be nice if it made sense, I thought. Later that day, I received a message from my client:

"You're not going to believe this, but when I was dropping my cousin's kids off at school today, we saw a raccoon run across the street in the middle of the afternoon! Do you think that's why the song about the raccoon kept going through your head?"

"YES!" I said, "It was definitely a sign for you. It kept hitting me in the face!"

A few hours later I received another message from her: "I couldn't believe my eyes. It came back! This is incredible!" And she included this photo:

I love this type of evidence in a reading because it helps keep the connection going between my client and the Spirit World. This woman now has something specific from her loved one as a constant reminder of that undying love that is always present.

Most people believe they experience signs and synchronicities from the Universe or their loved ones in spirit. I believe our loved ones in spirit, our guides, and the Universe send us many signs and validations if we are open to receive them. They can come in many forms but are always accompanied by a feeling—a popular topic among both my clients who are receiving readings from me and those who are just awakening to their own intuition. They have felt, sensed, and seen signs they feel are from specific loved ones and others from the Universe in general. A lot of people want to know how to recognize signs or receive more.

Once you are aware of—and engage with—the signs around you, you begin to understand the process and detach from the need to receive specific signs to sustain your belief in the Spirit World and yourself.

It's important to acknowledge that, while many people feel comforted and validated by signs and synchronicities, we want to maintain a sense of calm and detachment as the process unfolds. Over-focusing or constantly looking everywhere for specific signs can limit our ability to receive them openly. I don't believe there is a limit to how often we can "ask" for signs, but once we do, we need to allow the Universe time to respond. Being overly focused on a specific idea of the sign we want to see does not lead to seeing more signs. We create our lives from the present moment, from now. If we are constantly looking forwards or backward, we leave ourselves no time to experience the present moment in which we are able to connect with our loved ones who have passed, our guides, or the Universe.

My advice is to set your intention then go experience life.

When we receive a sign that our loved ones in spirit are around, guiding and supporting us, we usually get a physical sensation. Our bodies are like antennae for energetic, psychic, and spirit information and a lot of people say they get chills, feel a difference in body temperature or a general change in the atmosphere.

When we are experiencing something profound that expands our consciousness, we will *feel* it. It's not something we need to search for, and very often these signs are not connected to one person we've lost. They can be from the Spirit World, the Universe, or whatever greater power and source of love you identify with—you needn't have lost someone special to receive signs. Once we are open to recognizing signs, they tend to appear.

Signs, synchronicities, and validations of this kind are most likely to come to us when:

- we are struggling, need or ask for help
- when we are really "tuned in" and have asked for or are hoping for a sign
- when we are on the right path, want validation for hard choices we've had to make, are trying something new, going through a major change

- when we are learning about spiritual topics, or taking a leap of faith

Ultimately, signs and synchronicities appear to support you on your journey and let you know that you are not alone.

As a psychic medium, I often hear stories from clients and friends of how their loved ones in spirit are sending them signs, and I am often the one giving these messages.

> "Your husband says there was a bluebird outside your window just this morning that made you think of him."
>
> "Your grandmother sends you cardinals."
>
> "Sometimes you smell smoke when your dad is around you."
>
> "Your friend said he was there when you saw that eagle. It was beautiful and made you think of him."
>
> "Your Mom loves drawing your attention to pennies with the year you were born."
>
> "When your son is near you, he says you smell sunshine on your face; it's like you can feel his warmth."

My Story: Spirit Signs in Nature

I have always felt the presence of signs and also felt I had more control when I was in nature. Or maybe I should say that I felt nature and the elements of the natural world have always been conspiring with me and on my behalf. Especially when it comes to being outdoors, I have always had a sense that I could communicate with the sun, planets, earth, and animals. Because we had all types of animals throughout my childhood and spent a lot of time outdoors, this part of me was particularly welcome in my family.

While there were rules about how we should look and behave in public, there were almost no rules about being outdoors and befriending creatures and plants from our backyard. My mother was particularly encouraging of our witchy behaviors unless they veered too far out of the realm of normalcy and safety. I remember her distress at trying to remove permanent marker drawings from the back of my sisters' necks, but she was much more understanding after I explained that it was a game we were playing in the woods, and never pried further.

Such unspoken rules were passed down through generations of my family, shaping the way I lived my life. There was an expected way to behave in public and my witchy ways were to be hidden, private, or covered up. The importance of what other people thought is a narrative I've had to work very hard to change as an adult.

One of the reasons I am so passionate about creating safe, judgment-free spaces for people to develop intuition and mediumship is because we have already been judged enough. We live in a society that has not valued and appreciated our sensitivity. Organized religions and governments have historically kept apart people who have psychic and mediumistic abilities. Many times, we have shut down our sensitivity and hidden our abilities. To now live in a time where we can gather freely, and share is remarkable.

For purposes of practice and conversation within my classes, I have a very open mind—I honor and respect other people's beliefs. At the same time, I'm not for everyone and have healthy personal boundaries that honor and respect what I believe—I do not fear the Spirit World, psychism, or lots of fear-based projections. Beyond that, the only set rules for my practice groups are kindness, integrity, and authenticity. It seems when we are being kind and authentic, we have integrity. On that foundation, everything else falls nicely into place. Intuition is a natural ability, so we don't need a lot of rules and structure.

Most of the signs I've received throughout my life came through animals and nature. Perhaps it's simply how I am most comfortable receiving such signs. I know lots of people also find numbers significant and notice patterns. If you're willing to engage in noticing these types of things, they are all ways the Universe will conspire to let you know you are on the right track. The more I have become accepting of my true nature, the more I want to surround myself with plants, flowers, and—their natural energy and vibration is restorative to me. I've developed a routine and ritual for everything, from cleaning and clearing my home with them to helping me sleep at night. The earth's energy is a resource that we tend to overlook in the busyness of our lives.

As I write this, I know I have a ladybug living in one of the plants in my living room because it's too cold for me to let her outside. I feel the energy has shifted in that room since welcoming her into my home, and I like being aware of these things.

I have two teenage sons, and a few years ago one of them was hospitalized during a major snowstorm right around Christmas, which was devastating for our family. Our house felt so empty, and the energy was just that of grief...knowing we would not be able to visit, that the power might go out, and it was already difficult to get through on the phone.

I stood in our living room looking out our large bay window and saw three deer—they looked like two parents and a baby. They were just pacing back and forth in the cul-de-sac in front of our home. I had this strange feeling that I was looking in a mirror: the parents were clearly stressed due to the impending storm and looking for something. I called my then-husband and younger son to come and look. We all stood there, transfixed watching the deer in our neighborhood, all with the same thought: There are only three of us here but there should be four. We should be together right now.

The sadness felt unbearable. I wanted to reach out into the empty space in front of me where my other son should be. Not being able to be physically near him felt so wrong and went against every instinct I had as a mother.

I closed my eyes and heard the noise of a subtle energetic vibration running through my ears, my mind, and it felt as though it was wrapping around my heart. I felt that this rushing noise was trying to speak to me, so I answered with, "Please, please help me to see that what is happening is okay. It feels like too much."

Around me, I felt the atmosphere start to change. I felt more calm, peaceful, and loving. I felt a deep knowing that everything would be okay. I opened my eyes and noticed my son and Mike standing next to me in the window, still amused and curious about the deer. They seem to know this experience was special, but also sad.

Just then, a fourth deer, another baby, came running out of the woods. I felt a tingling throughout my entire body, and wanted to jump up and down and shout, "Look what is happening! This is a miracle! They have their baby back! Everything is going to be okay!"

My entire being rejoiced with this miracle and then I noticed the reaction of Mike and my son: They had tears in their eyes. They could certainly feel it too.

I took out my phone and started recording the deer. They stayed for another three minutes in front of our house...making plans for the storm, adjusting to the good news that they were all together, looking for which direction to turn.

I watched them walk down the end of our street and disappear into a neighbor's yard. Then I took a deep breath and asked, "What is the message here?"

"Hope," I heard. "You will be together again."

Still connected in this divine space of knowing, I did not question when we would be together again. I did not know if it meant in this lifetime or in spirit. I simply accepted this as the truth. We would be together again, and we were, and we are now.

It's taken me a long time to get to a place of complete trust with the Spirit World and to be okay with things not being okay. I'm generally a positive person. I hope things will be okay, and at the same time I understand that even if they are not, they will be broadly survivable. This is the version of positivity that works for me. I find comfort in knowing that I have no real control over most things at the same time it frightens me.

At the center of this journey to being okay with not being okay is mindfulness as well as my trust in the Spirit World. We create our life in the present moment when we connect to our intuition. It is always in the present; we never feel connected by worrying over the future or lamenting the past. Of course, it is human to do both these things.

However, by staying in the present, I am continually saying, "Yes" to the Universe and to myself. I am showing up for my life in the most meaningful way I can. This is something I have the privilege to choose, so I choose it again and again, in every second that I have the chance.

A few months later, my son was home from the hospital, and he was having trouble sleeping. He began going outside in the middle of the night for some air. As a parent, this terrified me, but I also understood his desire to break free because I had felt that way as a kid and had often snuck out of my house at night.

This night, my son started walking and was a few miles from the house when I woke up and realized he was gone. I noticed the screen was missing in the kitchen window and that his sneakers were missing from their usual spot in the front hall. I paced around for what felt like an eternity, continually looking out the front bay window where we had seen that family of deer a few months earlier. Thankfully, it wasn't long before I saw my son walking quickly up our street. I opened the front door and hugged him without saying anything.

"I walked really far," he said, "Then I suddenly got the feeling I should head home." He told me he started running towards the house but was stopped suddenly when he saw a young deer standing on the edge of the woods. "He was just looking at me," he said. "It was like he was telling me that it's time to go home now."

EXERCISE: GROUNDING TO CONNECT WITH NATURE

- Sit in a quiet space where you will not be disturbed
- Have a journal or notebook and something to write with
- Close your eyes and take a deep cleansing breath
- Start to notice the way your breath feels in your body
- Let yourself fall into a natural rhythm of breathing and notice the moment you begin to feel a calm, a stillness, or a connection

to yourself. As you feel your essence—your spirit—notice the energy of you.

Bring your attention to the bottoms of your feet, notice the subtle energetic vibration of the Earth beneath your feet. Wherever you are seated, the Earth is beneath you. Start to focus more and more on the energy you feel beneath your feet. The more you focus on this feeling, the more aware of it you will become.

On your next breath, inhale and imagine bringing the energy of the Earth up through the bottom of your feet, through your legs, thighs, hips, and into your heart center. Imagine this energy of the Earth blending with your essence, your spirit. Now, notice how you feel.

When you feel you've made this connection and are ready to bring your attention slowly back into the room, begin noticing your physical body again—wiggle your fingers, becoming aware of the sounds in the room you are in. When you are ready, open your eyes.

Journal about your experience:

- Perhaps you suddenly have become aware of something from your intuition?
- What does the energy of the Earth feel like to you?
- What does your essence feel like?
- How does it feel to blend the two?

8

My Story–Josh

From Friend to Spirit Guide

A few years ago, I attended a fundraising event that featured four notable professional mediums, including John Holland, who I was excited to see for the first time in person. John is a well-known medium from Boston whose books were some of the first I read on mediumship. His lighthearted and direct style combined with his Boston accent really spoke to me. But I wasn't feeling well that day and was questioning my decision to attend as I arrived at the hotel to see chairs packed tightly together for a crowd of almost 250 people.

When it was John's turn to demonstrate, I was impressed by his style. He began each contact with extremely specific details about the Spirit Person he was communicating with. I appreciated his willingness to be so specific in a large crowd. In his last contact of the evening, John began by saying that he had a young man with him in the Spirit World. He said he knew the young man had crossed over not of his own doing, but that he was taking some responsibility for his choices. He said he felt the man had a brother and sister, and that he'd struggled to pay attention in school. I started feeling anxiety creeping into my stomach as Josh came to mind.

John continued: "He loved animals, this kid. He has a dog with him. Several dogs actually. He's very active and jumpy. I can't hold still with this kid." As John started to bounce around the platform, it was clear to me that he was taking on some of the mannerisms of the Spirit Person he was communicating with. I started to feel Josh energetically nudging me and getting excited, and I began to sweat at the idea of standing up in front of this large crowd and speaking into a microphone.

"Now this is really unusual," John said. "This person must be in a glass urn. And not just any urn, but his face is etched into it. And you can see through it like a snow globe!" I was frozen in my seat and overwhelmed by Josh's presence, and sure that John was communicating with him. John continued talking about the snow globe and I looked around to see that no one in the audience was speaking up. A woman walked up and down the aisle with a microphone, waiting for someone to put their hand up so John could make his connection.

Suddenly I was on my feet. I saw the woman moving towards me, my friends on either side looked up at me with surprise. The woman passed me a microphone. Now John and everyone else in the room were looking at me.

"What's your name, dear? How do you know this kid?" John asked.

"Sheryl," I answered. "He was like a brother to me."

"Do you know about the glass urn? I need to make sure you know about the urn."

I answered, "It's not an urn, but it's on top of his grave-stone."

"No, no," John said. "This isn't a carving on a gravestone. This is unusual, like a snow globe." He started to look around the audience for the correct recipient and began drawing a sketch of the "snow globe" on a large pad of paper that was hanging behind him. The woman who'd passed me the microphone started to reach towards me, but to my surprise, I acted in a way unlike myself and ignored her.

"It *is* very unusual," I said loudly into the microphone, now feeling certain that someone else, someone pushy like Josh, was influencing me.

"I've never seen anything like it," I continued. "His mother had it designed. His face is etched in glass, just like a snow globe. The light shines through it during the day and it has a solar-powered light at night."

Suddenly, I had John's attention again. "Yes, that's it, I need to talk to you sweetheart."

I breathed a quick sigh of relief now that I could relax and let Josh take over. John went on to describe Josh's personality, his family life, his struggles in school. He talked about our vacations together in New Hampshire and how he had two dogs with him, one his and one mine. He knew that Josh had worked on cars, and he gave me several names of his friends and family.

"Make sure you tell his family that he made a big appearance here tonight," John said. "That's really important to him."

I would, of course, call his mother the next day and tell her everything.

Then John said, "Are you sure this kid was like a brother to you? It feels like more than that. Like you were in love. C'mon you can tell us," he joked.

"He was like a brother to me. We were very close," I said.

"He really loves you," John said, pacing back and forth on the stage, "It's more than love. He keeps saying to me, "This girl is my heart, this girl is my heart." John motioned putting his hands into the shape of a heart over his chest.

I couldn't say anything. I just tried to breathe as carefully as I could to prevent losing control of my emotions. I wondered why Josh was being so loving. Did he really feel all of that for me? "Yes," I heard him say in my mind.

We'd been communicating for the past seventeen years since Josh had passed to the Spirit World. Why, in this crowd of people who surely could use a message more than me, was Josh here in such a big way? Why was he making these profound statements of love towards me? Had I needed this reciprocation?

I started to feel a lump rising in my throat as I fought back tears that I feared would turn into uncontrollable sobs if I let them fall. "Please don't let this happen here," I prayed silently.

Suddenly I felt the energy around me shift and Josh seemed to be laughing. The reading wasn't over.

"Oh, there's one more thing, really quick," John said. "He wants you to keep singing."

Our song, maybe he means our song?

"I think I understand," I answered.

A memory of us as kids flashed in my mind. Me, Josh, and my sister snug in the back seat of a hot car happily singing together on the way to camp each morning. We sang the same song over and over that year "Happy Together" by The Turtles.

"I want to be really sure you understand," said John. "He says you used to be a singer, is that true?"

Oh! Now I know what he's getting at. "Yes, that's true..." I answered slowly.

"Well then, tell us about it!" said John with a big smile on his face, clearly sensing there was a joke here.

"In high school, I used to be a singer...in a Spice Girl impersonation group," I said sheepishly into the microphone.

The crowd laughed, clearly relieved to have a break from the emotional tension in the room.

"Wow, that's great," John said, smiling and shaking his head. "You can't make this stuff up. Only in Boston." He wished me well and reiterated how much Josh loved me, that he was always with me. I promised to call his mom the next day to tell her all about his big appearance.

When I reflect on the readings I received over the years, I am always curious why Josh—of all my passed loved ones—seems to come through in such a big way. While I don't have the complete answer, the relationship we've cultivated over the years since he's been gone from this earth has been one of the most important, constant, and loving relationships in my life, even though we've had our separate evolutions.

When he passed to The Spirit World, Josh was an emotional teenager acting on impulses and I was painfully shy and self-repressed. I've had quite the transition over the years. And, surprisingly, Josh has grown to be a teacher that I respect, an unconditionally loving Spirit Guide, and a lifelong friend. He has shown me he is able to express love freely and work with others in the Spirit World, and that part of his purpose now is helping people like him who have passed before their time come to terms with their new way of being.

Josh was only a year younger than me, but he was always a little brother in my eyes. We met after I dragged my mother over to his stroller when I was two years old. His mother and my mother became best friends, and we all became family. It's not especially remarkable that a shy toddler would drag her mother over to meet the neighbors and they would become lifelong friends. What is remarkable are the ways in which we've been woven together, not just as friends but as players in each other's destiny.

We never know exactly in which moments our life will change us. We can meet someone and in an instant, they can become the most important part of our world. People who we've known forever and rely on every day can disappear from our lives in that same space of an instant. This would be the case for Josh and me. He would be the most important person in the world to me—saving my life when we were children. Years later, I got a call from my dad letting me know that Josh was gone. I remember fighting to convince my dad he was wrong. But eventually, I had to accept that Josh was physically gone from all our lives.

Still, I had no idea he would continue to be a part of my life in so many ways.

That Time He Saved My Life

This deeper connection with Josh began when I was eleven years old. My family had moved to a neighborhood that was all new construction.

For a time, we were the only house at the end of a long road. The woods behind our new house were a protected nature reserve with endless possibilities for exploring, so I spent most of my time outdoors.

Being the only house on the street, there weren't a lot of neighborhood kids to play with, so Josh and his younger siblings would come over. On this day, Josh and I were supposed to be babysitting our younger siblings when we decided to head across the street alone to explore some new homes under construction.

I loved looking in the houses when they were being built and imagining who would live there. I'd picture what the future homeowners might be doing now and wonder how they'd feel about some strange girl being in the foundation of their house before it was theirs. Josh loved looking over the construction sites for tools that might have been left behind and finding new rock piles to climb. This day, it was just the two of us exploring because it had started to lightly rain, making the other kids want to stay inside eating cookie dough and watching a movie. (It turns out we were not very good babysitters at the age of ten and eleven.)

I had borrowed a pair of Josh's sneakers that he said would help me keep up with him. Clearly, he didn't want me to slow down this expedition and had figured it was just a question of footwear. In one lot, Josh started to climb to the top of a sand pile that was almost as high as the second floor. He called for me to follow him, but I just stood at the bottom, thinking about it. I imagined it might be nice to get to the top so I could look into the second floor of this new house. I wanted to see if their bedrooms looked like mine and imagine who would eventually live across the street from us.

"C'mon!" Josh yelled from the top of the sand hill, "Let's gooooooo!" He was getting impatient now, proud that he'd made it all the way up. He began strutting around, hands on his hips, wanting an audience. "I can see the whole world from up here!" he yelled, waving around a stick he'd found.

I started to climb up one side of the sand pile, which quickly proved to be a lot harder than it looked. I was sweating, covered in sand, and had barely gone a few feet when Josh looked over the edge impatiently but quickly looking away, knowing better than to laugh at me. I wondered how he had gotten up there so fast. It started to rain more, and the cold rain felt good on my skin, washing away some of the sand.

"Wow, look at that!" Josh yelled from the top of the sand pile. I couldn't see anything, but I heard a loud clap of thunder and a few seconds later Josh squealed with excitement. "I think it just hit a tree behind your house!"

He was having fun and I was grateful to have some time to finish my climb without him watching me. There were several large rocks emerging from the sand as the rain wetted it, and they helped me to keep my footing as I continued climbing the steep angle. When I finally reached the top, I was panting and exhausted.

Josh had lost most of his excitement by then, the novelty having worn off. Suddenly, though, the rain began coming down so hard I could barely see Josh who was only standing about ten feet away.

"Let's go back!" I yelled, sounding more afraid than I meant to. I started to feel disoriented, like the hill was falling or moving somehow. There was more lightning, and the rain pounded even harder. This is dangerous, I thought.

Josh yelled something at me, but I couldn't hear him. I started walking towards him, and noticed I had to pull really hard to get my foot out of the sand. Had I been sinking slowly this whole time? As I walked, I started sinking further. It happened slowly at first, and then suddenly I had to pull my foot out as hard as I could, losing one of his sneakers in the mud. Oh no, I thought. He's going to be so mad.

Josh had a temper and although it was never something directed at me, I wanted to avoid it.

"Stop!" he yelled at me. "Stop moving!"

I ignored him and kept going. But when I tried to pull my other foot out and lost his other shoe in the mud, I started to panic. I leaned forward trying to use my arms and chest to leverage my way out but wasn't getting very far. The rain was coming down so hard I felt like I was drowning. Half of my body was stuck in the sand, and the other half was soaked as water poured in my eyes and mouth.

I struggled hard, but the more I moved, the deeper I sank. Then I heard a rushing sound in my ears and felt a sense of certainty come over me. Suddenly, I knew I needed to be calm and still in that moment. I stopped moving, and I began to breathe very slowly. All I could hear was the rushing sound, my pounding heartbeat, and the breath going in and out of my lungs. I couldn't see Josh anywhere, but I knew he hadn't left. I closed my eyes to keep the sand and water from coming in and tried to ignore the fact that my entire body was beneath the sand and God knows what else might have been under there.

I had no idea what to do. But with my eyes still closed, something made me reach my arms and hands out straight as far as I could. Suddenly, I felt Josh's hands grip my wrists, *hard.* So hard that it shocked me, and I opened my eyes. I could see his face closer to me now and I saw his eyes looking right into mine. He didn't look scared at all. He looked like he was on a professional rescue mission, like he'd been training for this his whole life.

"Now you hold on to me," he said. His voice sounded nothing like the ten-year-old kid I knew.

I grabbed his wrists as hard as I could, and he started sliding backward towards his side of the hill. I felt my chest coming free and it was easier to breathe. Moments later, my legs were free. I first felt a rush of relief then a sudden panic as I realized that all of my clothing from the waist down had stayed in the mud as he pulled me out. We were at the edge of the hill, and it was still raining too hard to really see each other. I was thankful to be covered in mud, but I could tell he was purposefully looking away from me.

"I told you we shouldn't have come out here!" I shouted at him angrily, starting to make my way down his side of the hill—a much easier and steadier climb than the side I had gone up. I was furious and embarrassed. I ran past him into the house as he shouted after me, "Get back here! What about my shoes!?" But I just ignored him and kept running as fast as I could.

We feigned anger at each other for months after that and didn't speak about it until a year later when we were at his house. It was around the holidays and Josh was asking his mom to buy him the newest sneakers.

"Josh, you have so many pairs," his mom said. "What about those red ones?"

"Yeah, I miss those," he said, throwing a look in my direction, watching for my reaction. When I glared at him threateningly, his face fell into an apology. "That's okay," he said. "They probably wouldn't fit me now anyways."

That moment was the closest we ever came to speaking about our big misadventure. But I think about that day all the time—how calm Josh was, how focused, how completely capable he seemed for a ten-year-old. I felt guilty for never thanking him and wondered if he had realized how capable he truly was. Sadly, I don't think he ever did.

Together Forever

The day Josh died about ten years later, my dad called me at work to tell me the news. I was out in the middle of the used car lot at work, checking for a missing key but I could tell by the sound of his voice that something was wrong. So, I got into one of the cars, shut the door, and I braced myself for the news.

At the time, Mike, was deployed in Iraq and I was sure my dad was about to tell me something had happened to him or his unit. At first, I listened, relieved, as my dad explained that Josh had been at a friend's house and taken some pain medication. He passed out and, because of his asthma and the family's cats, his breathing had slowed. My dad wasn't sure if he had overdosed, had an asthma attack, or both.

"Okay," I said. "Did you go visit him yet? What hospital is he in?"

"No honey," my dad said. "He didn't make it. He died, Sheryl. I'm so sorry." I heard my dad start crying then he asked where I was; he wanted to come get me.

"I'm out on the lot, looking for a key. I'll call you back," I said and hung up the phone. Then I sat in the car in a state of shock. Every time I closed my eyes, I could see Josh's face. I could even smell him. The face in my mind was his face the last time I saw him.

I had driven him to go play golf with his friends and when he got out of the car, he'd awkwardly thanked me. I just said, "You're welcome, no problem!" in an overly cheery voice, suddenly trying to connect with him for some unknown reason. But I had a strange urge to give him a hug, although that wasn't something that we ever did. He would have laughed at me for suggesting it...wouldn't he?

As I closed my eyes in the quiet of the car, I felt his face against my face. He was wearing the white t-shirt he had worn to play golf. It was sunny and I could smell the sweat on his skin and his deodorant. It smelled like Old Spice or something, which always smelled strange to me as a teenager. *Is that what he smelled like?* I suddenly wasn't sure. I sat in that car going back and forth between grief and shock and what I thought was my imagination going wild, imagining him in the car with me. The next few months were a blur of grief and confusion, and we spent a lot of time with Josh's family.

Eventually things settled back into a normal routine. Work, writing letters to Mike who was still deployed, and going home to my apartment where I lived alone. I tried not to think about Josh. I had the feeling that if I thought of him, he would be able to see me, which made me feel awkward. I realize now that my own shyness was the only thing that had kept me from connecting with him during that time.

Christmas morning a few months after he died, I woke up sobbing in my bed. It wasn't that I felt sad, it was as if I could feel Josh's sadness. I could see him sitting alone and I could feel how much he missed everyone. It took me a long time to shake the feeling. By then, Mike had come home from Iraq, and we were visiting his parents in Ohio for the holiday. Mike suggested maybe I was missing my family as well, but I insisted that wasn't it. It was Josh. Josh was the one missing his family. This was his first Christmas without them. I kept telling Mike I could feel Josh's sadness. Finally, I had to let it go, and tried not to think about Josh.

This denial lasted until February when I found out I was pregnant with my first child. Mike and I were both working at the car dealership by then and enjoying living in the apartment I'd set up while he was deployed. I came home from work, opened a beer, and sat at the table staring at it.

"I think I might be pregnant." The words just popped out of my mouth.

"Really?!" Mike said, looking stunned.

"I don't know why I said that." I said feeling confused.

"Well, don't drink that beer then," Mike said suddenly, looking at me like I was fragile.

I got up, annoyed, and grabbed my keys and purse.

"Where are you going?" Mike asked.

"Well, if I can't drink this beer, I'm going to get a pregnancy test and figure this out."

As I drove to the store, I started intentionally talking to Josh for the first time. The idea that I was pregnant was so shocking to me, I lost my inhibitions and suddenly didn't care if Josh saw me. I felt like I was spinning out of control and reached for our connection to steady myself.

"Is this real?" I asked him. "Could you imagine if this was real, Josh?"

He wasn't answering, but for some reason I suddenly felt like laughing and that he was laughing, too—but it felt like a huff, like this vibration in my own chest, almost as if I was Josh laughing.

I parked and walked into the drug store feeling like he was walking beside me for support. His presence gave me so much confidence that I didn't feel embarrassed at all as I bought several home-pregnancy tests. As I went to check out, I recognized that I'd gone to middle school with the girl behind the counter.

"Hey Sheryl, how are things going?" she said, looking at the odd variety of pregnancy tests I'd chosen.

"Great!" I said then I saw Josh's face in my peripheral vision, laughing. I couldn't help it, I giggled, too.

Back in the apartment with Mike, he had his own fit of hysterical laughter as I revealed three pregnancy tests to him—he was going to be a dad.

For some reason, finding out that I was pregnant was the ice breaker I needed to connect with Josh. From then on, I felt more comfortable trying to communicate with him. When I would reach out to him for support, he felt different to me than when he had been alive. He seemed to have this wisdom that I didn't feel when he was here on Earth. The only time I had seen that side of him was when he had pulled me out of the mud pit.

Now it was like he was this wise, knowing person, and sometimes it made me feel uncomfortable—even resentful—imagining he thought he was superior to me. It was harder for me to connect with him when I felt that way.

Sometimes I would play "our song" from childhood that we used to listen to over and over on the way to camp, or "Happy Together" by the Turtles. Memories flooded through me of Josh, my sister Rachel, and I all squished together in the back seat, begging to play that song again and again. I remembered the lyrics about happy days and blue skies and that feeling that we would always be together. We sang it over and over that whole summer.

I thought about talking to Josh's Mom about how much I was feeling him around me, but I didn't know how to explain it. I was also afraid of having to justify these types of things. As a kid, I was accused of having an overactive imagination, looking for attention, or exaggerating. I couldn't always explain my strong reactions to certain people or situations, and this left me open to criticism. When others didn't understand the way I experienced the world, I blamed myself and assumed I was the one who was wrong or dishonest, which eventually led to keeping more of my feelings and experiences to myself. It had been a long time since I'd let myself be vulnerable to this sort of criticism and was reluctant to allow it again.

Around the time of Josh's birthday, I was driving home from work. I hadn't connected with him for a while. It was after I had my first son and I had emotionally shut down because of the medical trauma I'd experienced during his birth. I tried to avoid most feelings because I knew they could easily lead to panic attacks and flashbacks that would overwhelm me. I had just made it through October—my first son's birth month and Josh's.

Out of nowhere, I started to feel emotional and turned on the car radio, attempting to distract myself. Every station I tried was static. I looked to see if I had turned the radio to AM frequency and couldn't make sense why none of the stations worked. Frustrated, I turned it off, thinking it must have been broken. Then I heard static again and the lights of the radio flashed.

"Josh?" I said out loud for the first time in years. I started to feel uneasy as my emotions began to take over and pulled over to the side of the road. I turned the radio off again and again it turned back on. Static. Every station I tried was more static.

"Fine," I said out loud as I sat there, crying, and bracing myself for whatever was coming. Then I heard the words start to play through the static, becoming more and more clear: our song "Happy Together" began playing through the static.

I couldn't completely make sense of what was happening, but I knew Josh had figured out a way to control my radio and that made me laugh. I felt an overwhelming sense of him hugging me. Only this time when I closed my eyes, I felt like he was a little boy hugging me, a boy the age he was when we used to play together, before any awkwardness came between us. I sat there hugging him back for what seemed like forever and the radio played the rest of "our song."

The next day I called his mother, June, to tell her about it, because I knew that's what Josh wanted. She was very interested and understanding, and even said she'd had similar feelings of him.

Our relationship continued to develop this way for years. There would be days that I'd feel Josh with me closely, then weeks would go by where I didn't feel him at all. But not a day went by without a thought of him. These days, I feel him closest to me when I'm teaching mediumship or psychic development. Josh is usually the first to step forward to work with new students and will often chime in to help with my work—particularly if it has to do with kids or young people.

How My Son Met Josh

I will often practice with my kids the exercises I plan to use in my mediumship workshops. My youngest son is usually a willing participant and mediumship seems to come naturally to him.

One time, I handed him a piece of paper and wrote the name Joshua at the top. At this time my son was only twelve and I had not discussed Josh with him much. He didn't seem to recognize the name.

We set our intention to invite the Spirit World or Joshua to help us with this exercise. I asked my son to quickly write on the paper six words that came into his mind when he saw the name Joshua—he did not need to look for these words, he could simply allow them to come to him.

"Whatever comes first," I said.

He closed his eyes and took a deep breath. I smiled, admiring how he naturally knew how to do this and didn't seem nervous. On the paper he wrote "eyes, sad, school, dogs, cars, and adventure."

This has already worked out so much better than I planned, I thought.

I asked my son to go back to each word and take a breath with his eyes closed and be curious about what each word has to do with Joshua. "Don't try to figure it out, just let the feelings or information come into your mind."

He closed his eyes, took a breath, and said "Well, with the eyes, I could just see them. Like he was looking at me, and like he knew me."

I smiled and nodded. *Yes! This is absolutely working; he does know you!*

"Then, I felt like in his eyes he was sad," my son continued. "Like someone, maybe a teacher, wasn't nice to him. Like it was hard to be in school."

I suddenly felt so angry on Josh's behalf. He had ADHD but unlike me, was not the suffer-in-silence type. Josh was active, so active. Kind, honest, loyal, but could absolutely not sit still, and so was frequently misunderstood and dismissed. He was targeted by ignorant and uncaring teachers throughout his school years. I wondered what he could have achieved had he been able to channel that energy into something else... "I understand that" I said to my son.

"With the dog, I feel like he loves your dog Dusty, or a dog like him. Did he know Dusty?"

"Yes," I said. Josh had loved our childhood Collie, Dusty. I began to hear Josh's voice saying Dusty's name. Josh had also had a smaller version of Dusty of his own, a Sheltie named Sam. They were both with him in the Spirit World, along with the many other dogs Josh had known and loved.

Then my son said, "Yeah I feel like there are dogs all over him."

I smiled at that thought.

"I'm not sure about the cars," my son said. "Maybe I'm wrong about that." He was not completely immune to self-doubt, and after a certain amount of success, it had crept in.

"There is no such thing as wrong here," I said. "The cars are true. Take a deep breath and tell me how they feel."

He closed his eyes and took a deep breath. "I'm just seeing a lot of them, like downstairs outside at the dealership."

"Excellent!" I said, trying not to get overly excited at how well this was going. But I wasn't alone—I could also feel Josh's excitement at helping with this exercise. He had been a mechanic in his uncle's garage before he died, so the dealership made sense to me—especially the downstairs part where the service department had been.

"I don't really know about the adventure part," my son said.

"Was it a feeling you got?" I asked him, trying to discern how he'd been receiving the information. Then, I started to see what he'd been seeing: It looked like a movie, and I saw a young Harrison Ford running away from a boulder.

My son said, "Well it doesn't make sense, but I saw Indiana Jones, so I feel like that stands for adventure."

I have to stop and say here that "Well this doesn't make sense!" is perhaps my favorite thing to hear when someone is practicing mediumship or intuition. It's perfect in revealing the true connection because when something is coming to us from the Spirit World or our intuition, we don't always know how to make sense of it. Conversely, when it's coming from our logical mind, it may make perfect sense and that may be an indication that we've made an assumption or inserted one of our thoughts, hopes or desires into a message.

"Yes, I can see it too," I said, validating his Harrison Ford vision. Indiana Jones—that was Josh alright. He had certainly been epic when we were off exploring together and had even saved my life!

It wasn't until about a year after this exercise with my son that I was talking to June and this reading came up. I told her what my son had said, and she gasped. "SHERYL! That was his favorite movie! He had the hat, the whip! Wow, that's incredible!"

Josh, like every Spirit Person I've worked with, had an infinite intelligence, and presented information that was truly perfect. There can be so many layers to evidence both psychic and in mediumship, there are no mistakes.

9

Spirit Guides

You are Never Alone

We are all capable of cultivating meaningful connections with our loved ones who have left the physical world. The experience and ways of receiving connection and communication from them are vastly different for everyone, however, what remains constant is that love does not die. It is the powerful energy of our love that allows us our connection.

For those of us with loved ones in the Spirit World, we are waiting to be reunited with, having that promise of love and connection reaffirmed—whether it's through mediumship, dreams, or asking for signs—can be comforting. Our belief and trust in ourselves play a huge role in the results of this connection. Accept that these connections may be subtle. We may experience a feeling, a memory that suddenly comes to mind, or a song that plays on the radio, may begin to open the door to further our connections.

Know that your loved ones in the Spirit World are only a thought away and that you can ask them to be close to you. Know that when you speak to them, they will hear you.

Spirit guides are infinitely loving beings that are in our lives to guide, teach, and protect us. Regardless of their spiritual beliefs, everyone has spirit guides. Even if you don't see, hear, or feel your guides, you have them.

Not one person on this planet is alone in their life experience; we are all connected, guided, and loved.

When clients come to me wanting to understand mediumship and how to communicate with their spirit guides, I ask them to try to put into words how it feels when they are connecting with their guides. The answers are somewhat universal: more loving and more loved; like anything is possible; like they are coming home; like they are totally free and unlimited.

This is the power of the Spirit. We connect to our spirit guides not through our mind, but through our own spirit, and in this space, we feel different. When we are in our spirit we are unconditionally loving and free from many of the challenges we may face as humans.

When I am connecting with my guides, I am free of any judgment or unloving thoughts. Someone who has done terrible things can sit across from me and I can easily counsel and hold space for them without the intrusion of my own thoughts or feelings because I am under the influence of my spirit team. When we are working from our spirit, we don't assign meaning to things in the same way we do as our human self. There is no good or bad, only what is.

The Spirit World is as infinitely loving as it is intelligent.

You may not yet recognize it, but you are frequently connecting. It's common to want to rush the process of connecting to our guides, but when we try to rush the process, we invite our mind and our ego into the process. Our mind can easily invent an identity for our guides and our ego may also interject giving us a guide that we feel suits us or makes us special somehow. When you connect with spirit guides, try to keep your mind and ego out of the process, as it is a pure and authentic experience that needs to unfold naturally and without an agenda.

Every belief we have about spirit guides will act as our conditioning and ultimately shape or limit our experience. I was told by a spiritual teacher that once I learned more about spirituality and "ascended," I would meet otherworldly guides that were more holy and of a higher vibration than my current guides. She suggested one day I would speak directly to an angel as my guide.

That information about ascending and angels startled me as I considered losing the closest and most loving relationship I'd ever had and having to communicate with an angel. Growing up Jewish, angels were not part of my understanding and they do not resonate with me.

My main guide, who I have seen since I was a child, is very ordinary in appearance—a man with a hat and a mustache. When we first start connecting with our guides, we will likely find and experience a guide that is familiar to us and our experience. Especially when we connect with spirit guides as children, it is unlikely that the Spirit World would send us a guide who would startle or disturb us.

I also advise those beginning to connect with their guides for the first time not to share the specifics of their experiences too freely with others. Your relationship with your guides is personal, much like the relationship you have with yourself. Just as when you are first building trust in your intuition, the relationship may feel fragile. I encourage you to protect your growing confidence at all costs by not inviting someone else's ego or agenda into the relationship.

I have been in classes with teachers who told their students that they have a specific guide who is a famous person in history. Usually, though the student will be excited, they are often completely unaware of this guide, which can be damaging to their developing relationship. In some cases, people are left waiting to see a specific guide who may never appear to them because that guide came from the mind or the ego of another person.

As with all aspects of your spiritual journey, you are the ultimate authority. You need not and cannot outsource discovering and building a relationship with your guides to someone else.

There have been occasions when I will see something specific about a client's Spirit Guide and it will be in validation of an experience they have had. In a reading, I once told a young man that I saw a woman standing behind him in a long orange robe and I had a feeling that he had been communicating with her the evening before, asking for spiritual guidance. He immediately recognized the woman. Although he did not know her, he had a spiritual experience the night before when he saw her in his mind's eye. This is the type of evidence that is helpful to a client. Offering information on spirit guides without the evidence is not in alignment with my work because it cannot be validated, and I feel it does more harm than good.

My Story: Getting to Know My Guides

In 2017, when I began to open myself to mediumship again, I began to see the image of a man's face. He was very familiar to me from childhood, and easily recognizable by his mustache and the hat he wore. For some reason, as a child, I found this image very non-threatening and just assumed it was my imagination or some type of ghost that lived in my home. In my childhood imagination, it didn't really matter to me who that man was. As I got older, I started to fear this presence in my life made me different from others and wrong somehow.

Once I got up the courage to say to a friend, "I feel like I've gone an entire decade with someone watching me like I'm starring in my own TV series or something." There was an awkward silence. "Do you know what I mean?"

"I have no idea what that is," she said, looking puzzled.

This confirmed my suspicion that I was not like everyone else. It was years before I spoke about it again—this time to my therapist—and received almost the same response. "Maybe because of your loneliness, perhaps you made this up to feel safe, or you have a vivid imagination," she offered.

These were all explanations I accepted on the surface to be agreeable, but I feared they were not true. I assumed this was evidence of something else "wrong" with me, and that was easier to accept than the truth.

In 2017, the face of this man started appearing everywhere. I knew he was the man from my childhood—the one that had been present with me in the piano room and sat beside me while I escaped an abusive relationship. I sensed he'd been there with me during my near-death experience. I trusted him and the bond we shared.

We started communicating again, and his shadowlike, holographic face would appear all the time, everywhere. Objectively, I would see him anywhere I looked: in the sky, on the ceiling in the rafters, as I watched my son's basketball game, in the darkness before I closed my eyes at night.

One night, while watching a TV show with my ex-husband, I thought I saw the man in the TV show. I was stunned. This guy," I said, "this actor looks just like one of my spirit guides."

Mike didn't have much of a reaction. "Is that a good thing? Are you happy about that?" he asked.

I wasn't sure what it meant, but it felt good to share the information with someone who believed me and didn't seem alarmed by it. In the past, I always felt uncomfortable sharing this information for fear of being accused of making it up. Now his reaction gave me the confidence I needed to continue looking for answers.

I began sitting in meditation every day and asking the man questions. I didn't always hear his voice, but I could feel a sort of midwestern accent and had the thought that he reminded me of a relative from Utah. But that made no sense because I'd barely known this person. Still, the feeling of Utah was there.

During one meditation, I asked for proof of who he was and wanted to know his name. He spoke to me through my thoughts saying, "Go into the living room and when Mike asks you to do something, no matter what it is, say yes." My eyes popped open and suddenly my meditation was over, so I went into the living room.

It felt both strange and ridiculous as I went and sat quietly next to Mike, wondering what he'd suggest we do. When I remembered he had talked about wanting to clean out the garage earlier, I began to regret the exercise. I hoped he didn't suggest we wash the car. Mike looked at me suspiciously.

"What's up?"

"Nothing."

"Do you want to watch TV?" he asked.

"Sure," I said, relieved.

"What do you want to watch?"

"Whatever you want," I answered sincerely, curious to see where this would lead.

"Okay," he smiled, amused, and clearly picking up on some strangeness. I never wanted to watch what he wanted to watch. He flipped through some shows and settled on some reality rescue show about a woman who was trapped in a canyon for two days in the Utah desert waiting to be rescued.

"Do you really want to watch this?" he asked.

"Yes!" I said, eager to see where this would lead.

My interest was piqued at the reference to Utah and the accents sounded like they would match that of my guide, but it felt like a stretch. Then this sheriff appeared on the screen. He had a moustache and a hat. His name was John. I felt a little bit of excitement, like this was a sign pointing me in the right direction.

A few weeks later I attended a public mediumship demonstration with world-renowned Spiritualist medium, Mavis Patilla. I had dreamt about needing to go to this demonstration, and in my dream my grandmother insisted I bring my sister. All of Mavis's students demonstrated, and then at the end of the night she decided to have a connection of her own.

Mavis came directly to my sister and I with a message from our grandmother. Mavis shared very specific evidence, and we really felt our grandmother's presence. She even began to take on the mannerisms of my grandmother, moving and speaking like her. As she ended the reading she asked, "Who is a photographer? You brought the camera with you. You've got photographs to take." Mavis said to my sister who is a professional photographer.

Then she turned to me and said, "I know there's a John in the Spirit World. I don't feel family, but there's John." Another confirmation.

A few years later I went for a mediumship reading with one of my teachers, well-known spirit artist, Rita Berkowitz. Rita has the ability to draw the spirit people she communicates with, providing her recipients with portraits of their deceased loved ones as well as evidence.

When I'd made the appointment with her, I wasn't sure who she would draw but I hoped it would be one of my guides.

Rita began describing an intelligent and serious man with a very distinct moustache. I sat there, stunned, as her pencil moved across the paper creating the man's face just as I saw it in my mind. Tears streamed down my face; I couldn't begin to express how long I'd waited to have this validation. The fact that someone else could see what I saw gave me an immense sense of peace and relief.

Spirit Guide Drawing
By Rita Berkowitz

The gift that the Spirit World will bring to us—if we allow it—is knowing that we are not alone, that it's always been real, and is even more magical than we've allowed ourselves to believe.

I brought the drawing home, showed it to Mike, and we compared it to the photo of this "look-alike" actor. That was the proof I'd asked for. I felt confident in what I had been seeing; I knew it was real. After this experience, the face stopped appearing as often. I still feel the presence, but the objective clairvoyance seemed to have fulfilled the need that I had for validation and connection.

Now that I have a deeper understanding of my guides, I feel they use their energy to communicate with me telepathically and I can receive much more information this way.

Remember, when developing a relationship with your spirit guides, you are the authority on what you know. No one else can tell you who your guides are or what your relationship is. This is a deeply personal relationship, much like the relationship you have with yourself.

EXERCISE: BEGIN TO CONNECT TO YOUR GUIDES

*You can also say the Spirit World, God, Angels, the Universe ...whatever feels most natural for you.

- Sit in a quiet space where you won't be disturbed and have a notebook and pen.
- Set the intention to connect to your spirit team by using your own words to speak from your heart and simply ask them to be with you.
- Take a few deep cleansing breaths.
- Start to notice the pattern and rhythm of your breath as you begin to relax.
- With your imagination, visualize yourself seated outside, someplace you feel comfortable. Be very detailed about the scene. See the colors of your surroundings, every plant, animal, or tree around you, the details on a blade of grass.
- Inhale and notice how the air smells and how the air feels on your skin, how the warmth of the sun or cool breeze feels against you. Notice the earth, water, wind. Listen intently to every sound, chirping birds or rustling leaves on the trees. Listen to the silence.
- With your thoughts, invite your spirit guides to join you.
- Notice any changes in how you feel emotionally, physically, and in the atmosphere around you.
- Pay attention to subtle shifts in energy. You may see images or hear words or phrases in your mind.

After a few moments, thank your guides for being with you.

Journal about your experience.

After you've done this exercise a few times, you may want to change your intention to receive information or support from your spirit team. Your guides are always with you and want to support you on this journey. Many people want to connect with spirit guides for validation and answers during difficult times. Whatever your reason for wanting to connect, be clear in your intentions.

You can ask them for advice, guidance, love, support, and healing—signs that they are with you as often as you desire.

- Sit quietly in a comfortable place where you won't be disturbed.
- Have a pen and paper and any other items you like to use in prayer or meditation (a crystal, photo of a loved one, prayer beads...there are no rules whatever holds magic for you.)
- Set your intention for this session. If you are asking questions, try the following intention: "I ask Spirit* to be with me now as I reflect on the following questions to embody my highest self and live fully in my purpose."

Sit quietly for a few moments, focusing on your breath in the quiet. When you feel you are in the presence of your guides, open your eyes and ask the following three questions one by one.

- What is energizing me?
- What do I wish I had more time for?
- What am I most grateful for?

After asking the first question, immediately write down whatever comes to your mind (you can sift through after). Try to keep your writing momentum going and do not pick your pen up off the paper (it's okay to scribble, this is only for you!).

When you feel you are ready to move on, go to the next question and repeat the process.

10

Dreams

When we dream, we are most connected to our subconscious mind, our intuition, and our connection to the Spirit World. Dreams allow us direct access without interference from our conscious minds.

Many people look to dreams while they are developing intuition, searching for a deeper understanding of themselves, or wanting to connect with their own loved ones in the Spirit World. At times of stress or trauma, we are often more likely to remember our dreams. Whether it is our psychic awareness, our subconscious mind, or the Spirit World trying to communicate with us, all this information can be valuable. Keeping a dream journal helps develop an understanding of what's occurring.

Because I could easily track the connection between my dreams and waking reality, dream interpretation has both fascinated and terrified me since I was a kid. Now I love working with clients on dream interpretation as it's often a way intuition and psychic information presents. Subconscious fears and desires are also found in dreams, and for our sanity, it's important to know the difference.

There are many types of dreams and ways to decode information. For practical purposes, I'll talk about dreams in three categories: Psychic Dreams also called Premonition Dreams, Visitation Dreams connected to the Spirit World, and Standard Dreams, which will also include Vivid Dreams and Recurring Dreams.

Premonition Dreams

A psychic dream or premonition dream will predict future events or provide us with information that we may not otherwise have known through our conscious mind. Often, premonition dreams occur just before we awaken and remain fresh in our minds. We are also more likely to remember our dreams shortly before waking because each REM cycle is longer than the last.

I've experienced several dreams like this and it's one of the things that made me question if I wanted a close connection to my intuition—one time I even set an intention to no longer have such dreams. At the end of the chapter is an intention exercise for anyone struggling or distressed from these types of dreams or visions.

For me, this boundary became important in 2006 when I had a dream that my younger sister was attacked by a shark. I remember exactly the image of her washing up on the shore and the jagged rocks all around the beach. These dreams and images tend to be vivid and easily recalled. They are almost always accompanied by a strong feeling.

After waking, I picked up the phone at 6:00 am and called my mom to tell her my dream. Later that day, she called back to tell me that my sister had been attacked by a German Shepard.

It was a friend's dog that was recovering from illness and had become disturbed when my sister walked across the kitchen to throw something in the garbage can. As she got closer to the dog, she began to get an uneasy feeling and ended up tossing her paper from a foot away before slowly backing up. The dog lunged quickly, clamping down on her upper arm then retreated. After getting some stitches, she was, thankfully, okay.

My mom thought it could have been a lot worse had she not told my sister about my dream and that she was perhaps quicker to back carefully away from this dog when she sensed danger, rather than discount her own inner knowing or not wanting to seem overly sensitive in the presence of the owner.

That day, I promised to tell my family any more dreams I felt strongly about, but the whole situation left me feeling uneasy. I didn't want that kind of power or responsibility.

The next dream a few months later did not prove as helpful. I dreamed there was a pot of tomato sauce simmering on the stove at my parents' house. As I watched the pot simmering and eventually start to bubble over, I started to feel more and more distressed. It continued to escalate as I watched helplessly, it began to bubble out of the pot. The sauce started to fly and spatter and land on the floor and got on my parent's smallest dog, Ruby. Ruby was a tiny red teacup poodle weighing only three pounds and, I was frantically trying but unable to stop the sauce covering her tiny body. The other dogs in the house were tracking tomato sauce footprints all over the wooden floors. I woke up with an overwhelming feeling of dread again, so again, I called to tell my Mom.

That night, Ruby went over to one of their bigger dogs to boldly try and take a bone he was chewing right from his mouth. The bigger dog was gentle and playful, yet he refused to give her the bone. As he quickly switched his head from left to right, little Ruby, still stubbornly clamping on, was tossed across the kitchen floor. She landed hard several feet away and hit her head on the wood floor. Because of the angle and speed with which she fell, she died within minutes. My parents watched helplessly as the kitchen floor turned into a scene much like the vision in my dream with the tomato sauce.

I felt responsible somehow. After that, I set the intention for the dreams to stop. It was too much pressure.

I've come to believe that these dreams are not messages from the Spirit World, but rather from my own intuition and psychic senses. In my work with the Spirit World, they have never warned me of anything negative. They have only spoken in a language of love, with a wish to uplift and inspire us.

It's important to make that distinction as many people have a fear that if they begin to open to the Spirit World or their own spirit, they will become aware of "something bad that will happen."

"I don't want to know when I'm going to die" is a surprisingly common sentiment amongst my clients. Again, I offer this information so that you have the opportunity to feel how it resonates with you; if your soul has a recognition of the truth here, you may move on without that fear.

That said, many students and clients do—as I did—become more sensitive through their work with intuition and the Spirit World, and that can leave us open to knowing future events or having a sense of what's to come. This can be understood through time and practice, then used to guide us in living a meaningful life.

Recognizing when we have a dream that's going to be relevant to our life is part of developing intuition. In neither of the above dreams did I wake up feeling a strong sense of anxiety, just an urgency, a feeling, that this information was important but not really understanding how.

Developing intuition takes equal parts discipline and surrender. Meaning, we need to develop a practice of trusting ourselves, releasing our need to control situations and outcomes. If I feel I have a message to give someone close to me— my mom for example—I give that message, recognize that I've done my part, and release the outcome. Worrying constantly and calling to check in the rest of the day would drain my energy. Although I give into worrying thoughts and behaviors at times, in general, it is my practice to do whatever I need to, to set that energetic boundary, and let go.

Not all psychic dreams are negative. Very useful information will often come to me through a dream, which is one of the main reasons I like to keep a journal nearby.

Before I moved into my current home, I looked at another house I was very interested in purchasing. I told one of my closest friends, who is also a medium, about it. I was ready to put an offer in on the house. That night, I dreamed of my friend sitting around a fire at sunset in the middle of a marsh with tall grass and they said to me, "You're not going to buy that house. You're going to find a place that's only a mile from where you live now." When I woke up that morning, I knew very clearly that I was not going to buy that house and immediately put it out of my mind. It was that simple. My interest had shifted, and I knew that, for whatever reason, that house was not the right one.

When I looked at the dream interpretation, I took the marsh to mean "swamped or bogged down"; possibly the house would create that feeling for some reason. Fire is usually a symbol of passion, desire, or expression, and in this case, it was a carefully controlled campfire feeling. So, I sensed that it represented my own passion and creativity being controlled. Sunset can often represent the end of a cycle much like it signals the end of a day. The sun setting on my plans to purchase that house, moving from the home I'd lived in for fourteen years, certainly marked the end of a significant cycle.

The fact that my friend was the one giving me the message...This part was important as the people in our dreams typically represent other aspects of ourselves and often have nothing to do with them or their lives. When I think about this friend, the first thing that came to mind was that they are an extremely accurate medium. So, I took that to mean this was an accurate message I could trust. I scanned over all the pieces of the dream, and they felt true to the meanings I'd assigned. This entire process took me about three minutes, and I quickly decided not to put an offer in on that house.

A week later I signed a lease to rent a townhouse only a mile from where I lived, which gave me the freedom to reevaluate my living situation again when the lease was up. In the new place I rented when I look out the front windows, I see tall marsh-like grass planted around the front and side of the house exactly like in my dream. For me, this is just another example or validation of how information connects and can have multiple layers.

Visitation Dreams

Many people have visitation dreams—unique dreams in which our loved ones in spirit visit us. Two of the most common elements of these dreams are that they feel so real and that our loved ones are not angry, sick, or hurt. Instead, they are loving and whole and have usually come to us to let us know they are okay.

I used to have these dreams of my grandmother where I would hug her on the beach, I could feel the warmth of her skin and smell the oil she used. I could see in detail the side of her face and feel her take my hand. Things I'd forgotten about were suddenly back—like the shape of her arthritic curved hands in mine. I could feel them colder at the fingertips and warmer in the middle. I could see the yellowed ridges on her nails from having taken off the polish and lain in the sun. Even years later, these images are perfectly clear and easy to recall. Whenever I do, it's almost as if my grandmother were here.

This has always been the nature of clairvoyant images for me, and it's a good contemplating factor if I'm trying to help someone determine whether an image is coming from their memory or from the Spirit World. I very rarely have these dreams anymore—possibly because it's not necessary for me at this time in my life. In my experience, the Spirit World uses energy effectively to communicate. Perhaps, if I can communicate with them in other ways during the day, I don't need the dreams as often.

Standard Dreams

Standard Dreams can be just as valuable to us in receiving information from our subconscious as other types of dreams. There are many ways to begin interpreting and understanding our dreams. Looking at dream dictionaries and Googling symbolism is a good place to start. However, interpreting them intuitively will be the most accurate and helpful tool in the long run. Here are some common examples as you begin:

- Caring for an animal or baby is often about caring for an aspect of yourself. Consider how that care was being given, or not given.
- Driving a car typically alludes to your life's direction. Look at who was driving the car, was it controlled or out of control, how did you feel about it?
- Water typically represents emotion. Look at the clarity and color of the water and determine what that might mean to you. If you

were struggling to stay afloat with waves crashing over your head, or swimming in a lake with a murky bottom, that is quite different from relaxing in a bath or exploring a waterfall. Remembering how you felt is particularly important, because it will answer for you how this emotion is affecting you.

Recurring dreams are usually standard dreams that repeat throughout our life. Recurring dreams have been common for me, and often symbolize either an unmet need or frustration in my daily life. I also believe these dreams may point to overall themes in our life that can be helpful for us to recognize.

When I was a kid, I was always afraid of wolves. I had a difficult time going to sleep in the dark because I thought I could see a wolf's eyes watching me from anywhere I looked. I realized I had extreme light sensitivity when I was about eight, and that it was never really dark when I closed my eyes—it's almost as if the sensors keep firing, like a pixelated screen. I'm not sure why I started to notice and ask about this, but it was close to when my migraines started. When I closed my eyes, images would usually appear in the light behind them, and I would lay in bed watching the screen of whatever was happening.

What disturbed me the most was that I only saw the wolf when my eyes were open. I often had nightmares of being chased by this wolf. I would be running through the woods and then I would wake up in a panic. Interestingly, these dreams shifted for me a few years ago when I had a dream that *I was* a wolf and had the most vivid experience of running through the forest. I felt calm and free. When I woke up, I felt a little disturbed because the experience was so real, I felt I actually had paws, fangs, and a fur coat. It was a strange experience.

A few weeks later I was choosing a card from the Animal Spirit deck for a weekly tarot reading. When I do this, it's to connect with my own intuition. To get the most accurate and resonant messages, I ask my intuition what the meaning of each card is. For that card, the message I wrote was,

"To me the Wolf is the teacher, always invested in the greater good, humanitarian, activist energy. The mission of wolf energy as I see it is to create a sustainable and equitable world for all. While they appreciate humanity, the wolf sometimes has less appreciation for individual humans. The wolf sees and predicts problems before they arise and if you have a strong dose of this energy, you have likely been accused of "seeing issues when there are none.

That is not the case at all. It's simply that you have a keen eye for spotting issues before they arise, as well as a strong instinct and intuitive knowing as to when and how they will develop. When Wolf energy is at its highest expression, it is forward-thinking, inclusive, and brave. This energy is also prone to burn out and can become so forward-thinking that we become exasperated by the shortsightedness of those around us.

If you find yourself focusing on the actions or inactions of others, it's time to take a step back and release what you cannot control. Keeping your gaze forward and letting go will keep you in a more balanced space so you can do what you come here to do—create a better world for your pack."

Only after I wrote that did I start to think about the relevance to my dreams and see the symbolism in being afraid, as a child, of what I had now become. Some of the fears I had as a child now felt relevant—being a teacher, seeing issues others are unaware of, being a forward thinker, and being intuitive—now fit my understanding of self.

As in all things, if something feels relevant to you and you recognize the truth in it, you'll have a sense of knowing. This is your intuition—the most powerful sense you have in self-discovery. If something feels confused or out of reach, it's usually a good idea to put it to the side and trust that the information will come to you when it's meant to.

As you begin to develop your intuition and trust more, you'll also start realizing that your words, thoughts, and intentions are powerful. The simple intention of writing down what you'd like to happen can make a huge difference in how we experience the world. For one, it forces us to think about the result we'd like and be clear about it.

When I decided I didn't want to have any more precognitive dreams that predicted negative events, it was because I was pushed to the extreme and it was affecting my mental health. I was afraid to go to sleep at night because of what I might see or experience. By no means do we need to wait until we reach that point!

We can set intentions for anything we'd like. However, keep in mind that we don't have all the answers and it's best to leave some things open. When I ask to receive or not receive information, I will usually add something like "for the highest good of everyone involved," which communicates that I recognize and respect I do not have all the answers nor wish to control every outcome. I set my intention to stop these precognitive dreams at first by simply writing "I will not remember my dreams tonight" every night before I went to sleep, which worked immediately. If I forgot to write it down one night, I usually remembered my dreams.

The intention then became "I would only like to know and remember dreams as it serves the highest good of everyone involved." This was a bit of a disaster and seemed to invite all kinds of information coming to me about people in my life. So, no thank you.

Finally, it evolved to the winner (so far): "Let my sleep be restful and restorative, and may I only become aware of necessary, clear, healing messages while I am awake."

This intention is clear in that I'm projecting for my sleep to be restorative and restful, not leaving room for much else to happen there. If I receive messages while I am awake, I'm asking for them to be clear, necessary, and healing. This provides me with the assurance that I'm not going to receive information that doesn't have a healing or preventative quality.

EXERCISE: TIPS TO REMEMBER & INTERPRET YOUR DREAMS

- Keep a notebook and something to write with next to your bed.
- When you wake up in the morning—before doing anything else—begin the practice of writing down what you've dreamt about or what is fresh in your mind. If you don't remember your dreams, that's okay. Sitting quietly and feeling into what your sleep has been like can be very useful; just write down whatever sensations you feel.

Keep in mind that dreams are oftentimes connected to whatever we are experiencing in our daily life. If you're going through a period or stress and trauma, your dreams are likely to reflect that, and you may not want to spend a lot of time or energy interpreting them. It may be more useful to care for yourself in other ways.

Sometimes, I use the note section on my phone to keep a log of dreams. I like this method because it allows me to search by date for dreams and impressions I have had. Looking backwards, almost all our impressions will be relevant. These notes help us begin to recognize what our intuition feels like. When you have a feeling about something and it's proven accurate from your notes, you will begin to put more and more trust in your intuition. Then when something doesn't make sense, it becomes less important because you will begin to trust that, eventually, everything connects.

3

Part Three

Tools for Connecting—How to Go Deeper

11

Creating Altars

Creating a home or space that helps you feel like yourself is an important part of cultivating your intuition. One of the simplest things you can do is set up an altar.

An altar is the energetic center of your home, where you can call on, or call in, your spirit guides, loved ones, or inspiration from the Spirit World. Think of your altar as an extension of your energy.

Altars have been used by nearly every religion since the beginning of time. As humans, we are naturally predisposed with foraging instincts from our hunter-gatherer origins. Even if you haven't thought about it before, gathering meaningful objects to display in a dedicated space may feel natural to you. Altars may be non-denominational and are a natural way to bring the energy of your hopes, dreams, and intentions into the physical realm.

As someone on a spiritual journey, your altar can help to focus your intention, manifest what you desire to bring into your life, ground you, and connect you to your physical space.

All you need is a dedicated space, like a small tabletop or even a bench. Let your intuition guide you in creating this space, making it as elaborate or simple as you desire. As you're setting it up, think about what you'd like to call in or release.

Setting up an altar in a new space helps change the energy and makes it feel like your own. Every living thing on your altar has its own energy and can influence its surroundings. The vibration of your plants and crystals stretches beyond the physical world into the energetic realm. It will change the feeling of your space. Whatever you choose to place on your altar is personal to you. Make it your own and be free with it.

I tend to organize my altar to include all four elements: water, fire, earth, air. I add items to call in the presence of my loved ones in the Spirit Realm, also adding anything that aides my intention-setting for the day, week, month, or year.

After my divorce, I moved into a place of my own for the first time in almost twenty years and my altar became essential to me in connecting to the energy in my new home.

When I set up my new altar, I chose objects I knew would bring in the energy I desired. For my new space, I added dried and fresh flowers for vitality, photographs of my grandmother and great grandmother for protection, and seashells I had collected the summer I made the decision to officially divorce and tell my children I am gay. To me, the shells held the bravery and strength of that decision.

I filled a jar with moon water and surrounded it with dried rose petals and rose quartz for self-love. I had long held an intention of the kind of partner I wanted to attract into my life and could feel the presence of someone coming towards me from the future—someone serious who would also bring a lot of joy. I put a painting of The Sun tarot card in the middle of the altar, as I felt this energy was warm and energetic like the physical sun. Next, I placed some items that reminded me of my childhood on the altar—pottery I had made as a kid and a small painting.

It felt perfect, like I was held as both a child and as a newly single adult.

Getting Started with Your Altar

When you begin to create an altar, start with foundational items.

These are often items that represent each of the four elements; items that invite in ancestors or the Spirit World.

I currently have many items on my altar that call in the four elements, though I often change them up to bring in the energy I need at that time. Begin with items that resonate with you, knowing that you may swap them out whenever it feels right.

Some ideas for items you can include on your altar to represent the four elements:

Fire

- Candles (a variety of colors)
- Incense
- Herbs for burning and smudging (rosemary, lavender, juniper, bay leaves, sage*)

*A word on white sage:

Smudging with and burning white sage is a sacred ritual of Indigenous people, for which they have historically been persecuted, and this practice has been culturally appropriated by people who do not value the sacred nature of it. With the rise of spirituality in the west, white sage has been overharvested and sold by unethical sources. If you plan to sage, I recommend researching and finding an ethical source (Indigenous-owned business) from which to obtain this herb.

An even better alternative is to find other herbs that are wonderful for clearing your space. I recommend researching your own culture to connect to clearing practices that may feel like home to you. For example, in my Jewish culture, burning herbs, throwing salt in the doorway, and hanging rosemary in the kitchen are common ways of clearing and purifying energy. Doing this helps me to feel connected to my ancestors.

Earth

- crystals and rocks
- animal bones
- tree bark
- bowls of salt or sand
- fresh or dried flowers

Water

- seashells
- river rocks
- a bowl of moon water*

*moon water: leave a bowl of water out the day and night of the full moon, charging the water with the moon's energy. You can then use this water to cleanse crystals and infuse your altar with intention.

Air

- feathers
- tarot cards
- poetry
- ideas

To call in ancestors, guides, or loved ones in the Spirit World

- photographs
- family heirlooms
- important objects from your childhood

- hair or ashes from a beloved pet

On my altar, I have included many personal objects such as my grandfather's compass, locks of my dog's hair, my grandmother's Star of David, and pottery I made as a kid. Each of these is important to me and helps me feel most like myself. Continue to add items to your altar as you feel guided by your intuition to do so. After a walk in the woods, for instance, I might bring home a river rock or feather and add that.

Setting Intentions with Your Altar

Anything you want to call in or release can have a working space on your altar. Bringing new items to your unique altar is a way of setting intentions for changes you wish to make in the physical realm.

I often use Tarot cards as an intentional tool. While the origins of the Tarot are unknown, it's believed they have been around since ancient times and are linked to ancient Greece, the Kabbalah, and the Romany people. My Tarot deck feels like an extension of my energy—a living force that asks to communicate and cards that beg to make themselves known.

When considering cards for your altar, it helps to understand some of their fundamental meanings. The Tarot typically has 78 cards that begin with the Major Arcana, followed by the Minor Arcana, the suits of swords (air), pentacles (earth), wands (fire), cups (water). The Major Arcana are twenty cards, beginning with The Fool, and follow his journey as he meets and collides with every facet of human existence from The Magician, Death, The Tower, ending with The World.

Tarot Cards to represent various intentions:

- Call in more love: The Lovers, Two of Cups, Four of Wands, Ace of Cups
- Call in joy: The Sun, The Star, Ten of Cups
- Manifest abundance: The Magician, Ten of Pentacles
- Connect to your intuition: The High Priestess

Oracle Cards are another divination tool you may want to include on your altar. These cards are free-flowing and don't typically follow a prescribed set of rules or order. Choose the ones that draw your eye and feel good to you. I have cards that simply contain one word like "authenticity," which is useful in connecting to intuition and our authentic self, or "visible," when working through anxieties around being seen or vulnerable.

Just like with Tarot, place the Oracle cards on your altar that speak to you or embody your intentions. As I finish writing this book, I have a card on my altar that reads "little by little."

Develop a spiritual practice that supports your intentions

- Sit in front of your altar for a few minutes a day and speak your intentions out loud as you light the candles. Periodically replace the water, salt, candles, or incense.
- Burn herbs to cleanse your space or spray herb-scented water to intentionally clear the energy of your altar. As you wave the smoke around (with a window open nearby), state your intention to clear the energy. When the energy feels clear to your intuitive self, it is cleared.

Your altar is for you to connect, and it represents your unique hopes and desires. Make this a safe space, a non-judgmental place for you to express your desires.

Let yourself be free with it—you make the rules.

Casting Spells with Your Altar

Spells are just another way of being intentional with your altar. Some collections of items I use on my altar to cast my own spells for specific outcomes or intentions are:

Items for calling in self-love

- rose quartz
- pink taper candles
- dried rose petals

Items for manifesting spiritual or financial abundance

- citrine
- a goat's horn
- turkey feather
- coins or paper money

Items for protection

- a porcupine quill
- black salt
- a family heirloom (I have my grandmother's pendant)
- river rocks
- petrified wood
- peat moss
- charcoal

For intuition

- purple taper candle
- labradorite
- amethyst
- dried herbs
- owl feather
- crow feather

For creativity

- dried or fresh flower bouquets
- orange taper candles

- artwork or photographs that inspire you

Find items that feel like home to you and create something unique.

Using Color on Your Altar

I encourage you to consider the use of colors as you set up an altar. Understanding and connecting to the world around us can help create a space that feels supportive. Just as we are connected with every living thing, the shapes, colors, and symbols that surround us in the universe affect us. The more we understand and connect to symbolism, color, geometry, numerology, astrology, the more tools we have to understand and interpret our experience. I have always been very visual, and color plays an important part in the way I set up any altar or sacred space.

Color Theory is the science and art of using color as well as understanding the way we, as humans, perceive it. Every color has a unique vibration. When we perceive the vibration of a color, our minds communicate messages about this color that is unique to us. Every color will reflect light differently and will, in turn, be perceived differently by each person.

Our life experiences influence the way we see and interpret color, and I find it useful in interpreting energy. If you struggle to put experiences and emotions into words, color can be a tool to help bring your feelings into your conscious awareness.

Notice what colors you are drawn to and what emotions you experience with various colors. Some of these associations will be shared by many people. For example: white is often associated with purity and cleanliness—a doctor's white lab coat, tablecloths in fine dining restaurants, sparkling white teeth. A person dressed in all white gives an impression of cleanliness or status—they are certainly not planning to sit on the ground or take public transportation or devour a substantial meal.

When my kids were young, I worked in a fine dining restaurant and my uniform was a fitted white chef's jacket. When I sometimes put my jacket on at home, I noticed the difference in how my children instinctively treated me—standing on their tiptoes, pressing their lips out, and balancing only their fingertips on my arms were signs of respect for the cleanliness of the jacket. An ironed white jacket makes an impression, even to babies.

There are unlimited ways in which we can study color as it relates to us psychologically. For the purposes of exploring intuition, simply noticing color and what it means to you helps you receive more information. Be curious about the colors you choose to wear. Look at the people around you and imagine the color of their energy. Be curious about the colors you notice in the world and in nature.

When I met and fell in love with my partner Rachel, she kept remarking on how many pink trees bloomed in the spring. Everywhere we went she commented, "There's another one! Was I missing these before?"

We met after a somber year in our each of our lives. She had experienced the deaths of her grandparents, a painful breakup, and was forced to move from the apartment she loved—all within a six-month span. I was newly separated and living on my own for the first time, which was exciting but also strange. We had both separately taken up the hobby of walking in and exploring cemeteries. After we met, we began doing this together.

One day we were walking by a particularly beautiful flowering tree and Rachel stopped to take out her phone. "I have to see if this was here before," she said as she looked through her photographs from last year and saw that the tree had been there all along. "I swear I never noticed it before, but everything is pink now!"

I shared with her that I had started noticing yellow everywhere and pointed to our surroundings—a yellow bush and daffodils lining a pond. To her surprise, there was just as much yellow as pink. On the drive home, when she pointed to the pink, I pointed out the yellow to match.

After sharing the ways we both were noticing new colors, I said, "I feel like I'm noticing the yellow now because of joy. It's like my soul is seeking it out at every turn telling me, "There is joy for you, enjoy it."

Rachel is a serious and analytical person. She likes things to make sense and fall into a natural order that can be understood. She is reserved in her beliefs, strong and independent in her opinions, and extremely risk averse. She listens when I talk about mediumship and accepts that what I tell her is true for me.

As much as we have in common, we are equally different in our philosophies. I have a spell cast on my house for love, light, and peace and Rachel has lock reinforcers, a fire extinguisher on every floor, and a ladder to climb out of the bedroom window in case of fire.

Rachel thought about this and agreed that our brains could be drawn to and notice certain colors based on our moods and psychological states. "Last year, everything was so grey," she said. "The pink could be because everything in my life is so much better now; I'm happier and I feel like I can be myself."

"I always associate pink with self-love," I replied.

She pulled me close and whispered in my ear, "I am so grateful I met you."

Imagining what color you'd like to bring into your life, and the corresponding feeling or experience that you associate with that color, helps your manifesting practices. Find items in those colors and add them to your altar.

A Word on Crystals

All over the world, occultists, seekers, and mystics admire and collect crystals. They are one of the easiest ways to bring something beautiful and living into your space. They are alive, and like plants, have an aura—an energy that can be felt by highly sensitive and intuitive people. Crystals not only enhance the beauty of a space, they are healing.

We don't need to invest money into crystals, plants, tarot cards, or expensive items. Your intuition and innate wisdom are not dependent on the presence of a crystal. They are simply a beautiful yet optional part of complementing your physical space. Let your body and intuition guide you towards what feels right for you.

EXERCISE: CHOOSING ITEMS FOR YOUR ALTAR

The following exercise will help you begin to rely on your intuition as you connect with your altar. Once you are practiced at feeling the energy of an object and listening intuitively to how your body, mind, and spirit responds to it, this practice will become second nature to you. You will be able to pick up an object in a store or on a walk through the woods and know immediately if it will be a good fit for your space.

- Sit in a quiet space where you won't be disturbed and have some items with you that you are considering for your altar.
- Notice what colors you are drawn to and ask yourself why.
- Pick up one of the objects. Close your eyes and take a deep breath. Feel the energy of it in your hand.
- Put your hand on your heart and allow yourself to feel the essence of the object.
- Notice how your body feels and notice the difference in energy between you and the object.
- If it could speak to you, what would it say?
- What energy does that crystal inspire within you? Joy, peace, tranquility, grounded protection, innovation, self-care?

Place any objects that feel supportive on your altar and discard or put aside anything that, at this time, does not.

12

Using Tarot to Connect to Your Intuition

While the origins of the tarot are unknown, it's believed to have been around since ancient times and linked to ancient Greece, the Kabbalah, and the Romany people. I have a deep relationship with tarot, and my deck feels like an extension of my energy, a living force that asks to communicate, and cards that beg to make themselves known.

But this was not always the case. As a kid, I was both curious and fearful of tarot. When friends or family members would have cards out, I would look away, afraid of what I would see and worried that I'd become aware of some terrible fate of someone I loved. It's also a common fear amongst clients I work with who are unfamiliar with tarot.

I now know the cards are a mirror of our current energy. The cards will reflect the truth of our situation and point out possible ways forward. Tarot will show you what challenges you will face, what you need to let go of, and where you should focus your intention.

When you first start to build a relationship with the tarot, think of it as a conversation with a trusted mentor or your higher self. There is no judgment or "negative" or "positive" messages in tarot, only the reflection of energy and an opportunity to find a way forward through self-knowledge and an understanding of circumstances. The best way to receive information is to remain as unattached as possible.

My fearful relationship with the tarot changed after I began to develop my mediumistic abilities. Once I found a deck that I connected with and started incorporating tarot into some of my intuitive readings, I very quickly learned that I could rely on the messages and accuracy of both the cards and my intuitive impressions that came with them. And I began getting regular tarot readings myself, which I highly recommend to anyone looking to deepen their connection with these mystical cards. Seeing how other people read and interpret the cards is a great way to gain a deeper understanding of the process.

As you practice, you will automatically develop your own style of reading and interpreting the cards.

Getting Started with Tarot

When it comes to choosing a deck, there are many options and artists that depict diverse bodies and identities through the imagery. I recommend looking online or at your local holistic center and choosing a deck with artwork that resonates with you. The one I use is an indie deck called The Fountain Tarot, created by the artist from oil-painted images. It has a modern and dreamy appearance, and the imagery feels like home to me.

I don't believe it matters which deck you choose, as long as *you* choose it and it's an authentic deck created to be a divination tool. One of the best readings I've ever received was from a woman who used a deck of playing cards.

Just like with traditional playing cards, the suits have some cards with people on them. Like all divination tools, they serve as a mirror for self-reflection and deep discovery. Beginning to practice and become familiar with the tarot is often of interest to those looking to dive deeper and connect to their intuition.

Simply choose a deck that speaks to you. Some superstitions say you need to be given a tarot deck to begin; this is untrue. Buy your own deck and take your time getting to know it. Build a relationship with your tarot deck and allow it to guide you slowly. When you get a new tarot deck, the objective is to infuse it with your energy, and become familiar with its energy.

To Begin Connecting with a New Tarot Deck

- Gather your favorite crystals, rocks, dried flower petals, herbs, and a candle.
- Clear your space by burning herbs, spraying a clearing mist, or use your energetic intention to clear and connect with this new tarot deck.
- Light a candle with a match.
- Set up your ritual objects in any way that feels natural to you. If this process feels silly or forced, give your inner child free rein to play and explore— there are no rules!
- Once you have your objects arranged, take your cards out and begin handling them. Imagine integrating your energy with them. Turn them over without asking questions, look at them, explore the images and symbolism. Turn the cards face down and notice how different cards feel when your hand passes over them. Try to intuit which type of cards your hand is touching then turn them over to see how your impressions were accurate.
- Place your dried flower petals in a dish or tray and submerge the cards in the petals.
- Hold your hands over them as you say out loud your hopes and dreams for self-exploration and work with this new divination tool, your new tarot deck.
- When you feel you are finished with your ritual, you are finished

Put your deck in its new place. Choose something that feels right to you, as a special cloth to wrap them in, a leather satchel, or a box.

Tarot as an Intuitive Tool

Once you have connected to your deck, begin using it to explore your intuition. While there are tarot readers who purely read the meanings of the cards, most readers use their intuition when interpreting meanings. In fact, it's hard not to.

Tarot is an intuitive tool. Tarot cards provide structure and inspiration for your intuition because the rich imagery is a great jumping-off point for receiving messages. By simply wondering what each card means, you will invite your intuition to provide context by communicating to your intuitive senses. This may happen through images in your imagination, feeling, sensing, or knowing meanings—or even hearing words in your mind.

There is so much symbolism and meaning in a tarot deck, that as you draw cards in answer to questions or queries, the Universe will always take the opportunity to respond and provide you the answers you seek. Then it's up to your intuitive senses to take over. As you practice reading tarot for yourself, you will begin to trust the cards and messages you receive, which will help you build confidence and trust in your connection. You will start to know and believe in the power of not only the tarot but your own intuition. There is ancient magic connected to tarot, and the more you believe in it, the easier it becomes to work with.

Learning the traditional meanings of each card takes time and practice. However, in understanding these meanings you develop a valuable tool for divination and self-discovery. Though interpreting the meanings intuitively is important, learning the traditional meanings adds a magical reference system to your intuitive work.

The best way to get to know your tarot deck is to start a daily practice. By taking time to reflect or journal over the cards you can begin to gain a deeper understanding of their many meanings.

How to begin a daily practice:

- Set your intention. By making your it clear and specific, you send a powerful message into the Universe for your desired outcome. In the beginning, your intention may simply be "to connect with the tarot for intuitive development." This is a great place to begin, and your intention can change over time.

- Formulate a question. For daily practice, you might ask something like, "Where should I focus my intention today?"
- Shuffle the cards in any way that feels natural to you. When you feel you are ready to stop, stop.
- Pull two or three cards. You may choose cards from anywhere in the deck, or right from the top.
- Before you look up the meanings, start by noticing the symbolism and imagery on the cards and what your eye is drawn to. What colors stand out to you? If one of your cards has a face on it, imagine what this person wants to say.
- Close your eyes and take a deep breath. "Tune in" to the meanings of the cards one by one and write down your impressions.
- Notice the similarities and differences between the cards. If you've chosen face cards, what would they like to say to one another?
- After you've finished receiving intuitive impressions, look up the traditional means and compare your information.

Most likely, what you've received will be in line with the meaning of the cards. Value your intuitive impressions as much as you do the card meanings. If something doesn't make sense to you at the moment, put it aside and trust that it will in time.

It's important to keep fear out of your practice and remain as open as possible. Remember, the tarot is not a tool to predict harm, but a tool to help you navigate your situation, to bring you hope, and show you a way forward.

EXERCISE: JOURNALING WITH TAROT

Your words are an extension of your energy. Writing intentions and journaling can be a powerful tool in creating your reality. When journaling, I like a simple three-card spread for mind, body, spirit.

Pull three cards for each and lay them out face up.

- Card 1 is your Mind: I think of this as a surface layer, where your thoughts and personality are.
- Card 2 is your body: this is an inner layer—your body is a powerful messenger in communicating your feelings. How something feels in your body is important information to have.
- Card 3 is your spirit: here you move beyond the personality and thoughts and go within to listen to your inner guidance. This card is reading the energy of your spiritual self, what you would ultimately want and need without considering fear or outside influences.

Journaling prompts for connecting with yourself.

Use your breath to connect to your intuition and ask yourself:

- What does my inner world look like?
- What is needed to bring my dreams into reality?

Then pull one, two, or three cards per question.

Journal your impressions.

13

Seeing Auras and the Energy of Others

The aura is a unique energetic field that surrounds every living thing. Auras can be seen, sensed, and felt; they can expand and contract. Your aura holds the essence of your energy as well as experiences in the past, present, and future. As a highly sensitive or intuitive person, you have been sensing and reading auras your entire life.

Close your eyes for a moment and think about someone in your life who could be described as having a lot of energy or a "big presence." If you were at home and this person walked in your front door, would you know right away what kind of mood they were in or what their emotional state was?

For me, this is my dad—energetic, bold, passionate, a salesman at heart. If he walked in my front door the energy in my home would change. Some days, his aura sparkles like an electric current. I can feel the busyness of his thoughts, ideas, and plans for the day. When he's speaking to his sales team, his aura fills the entire room—everyone is essentially sitting in his energy. If he's positive and excited, the room becomes uplifted and motivated. If he's angry and disappointed, he could bring down the entire team. Before the team walks into a meeting, they are bracing themselves—some of them excited, some avoidant—but all of them will feel his energy in that room.

Now, think of one of the more reserved people in your life, perhaps someone introverted or shy. If they walked into your home, you may not register their presence right away. You may have to go and find them, ask how they are, really listen, and observe to get a feel for them. I often use my oldest son as an example of this type. When he comes home from school, I need to ask the right questions and listen between the words of his responses. Once he begins to open up, I can tune into his energy, though I will often need to hug or be close to him to know how he's feeling.

As you cultivate your intuition, you may begin to not only see auras but also feel them.

Auras were first popularized and linked to the chakra systems in the early 1900s. Early Hindu and Buddhist teachings explain chakras as life energy centers in the body. While many New Age teachers use the seven chakras to teach psychic and mediumistic work, it's not necessary to know the chakra systems to access our psychic and intuitive abilities. I have not studied chakra systems, yet I see and sense the energy of others. And like many highly sensitive and intuitive people, I can read auras without co-opting other cultural teachings. *

*A word on cultural appropriation: Western New Age spirituality has many places where we pick and choose sacred teachings and practices from other cultures—many of which have been historically oppressed or restricted—and make them a trend. This may be hurtful to generations of people who have suffered to preserve their traditions only to see others outside the culture dilute or profit off them.

How to Begin to See

Many people will be able to see auras by simply relaxing their eyes and looking "through" a person, animal, or plant. This often looks like a faint white line around the head and shoulders, and the moving energy can look like steam coming off of a hot grill in the summertime. You may notice that you can see an aura and can see *through it* as well.

In one of my aura workshops, I had a student sit in front of a blank white wall facing all the other students. I instructed the class to look through her to the wall behind, observe her aura and look at the energy waves surrounding her head and shoulders. I asked the student to relax into a happy memory and played an emotional piece of music. Everyone in the class observed her aura expanding—some noticed it becoming bigger and some saw it becoming brighter. Some of the students shared that they had observed colors and I asked them to feel into that color and the meaning of it. It was an empowering exercise that left everyone feeling excited to discover how natural it is to see auras.

Mediums and psychics often interpret auras through colors. Some people see color with their physical eyes, but we don't need to actually see a color to know it's there. You may see color clairvoyantly (in your mind's eye) or you may feel color with your intuition.

When seeing clairvoyantly, the color will feel like it's in your imagination. When feeling colors with your intuition, try to move the conscious mind aside and go with the first impression you get; you will get better with practice. In both instances, it's important to trust yourself and have patience. Many people feel like they are "making it up" and "just imagining things" when learning to do this.

For the next exercise, I asked half the class to stand on one side of the room and the rest on the opposite side so everyone was facing each other. Then they walked slowly toward each other until they could feel their partner's energy. Once they both said they could feel it, I asked how it would feel to take a step closer. Most people answered honestly that they would not want to step closer, and some even felt it would be almost impossible to do. When we are in tune with our own and another's energy, the instinctive feeling of keeping our own energetic boundaries is hard to ignore.

In one instance, two students said that they could not feel one another's energy and that there had been no change when they walked closer. Knowing that one of the students tends to project her aura all over the room, I asked everyone to sit down so this pair could have more space. Then I had them separate again, this time to the entire length of the room. Once they did, they immediately felt the difference. Because one person's aura was so expanded, they had been in one another's energy the entire time.

I typically see auras with my physical eyes but will tend to only see colors when I become curious about them when I am working, or in a mediumistic state. To me, reading the aura is one of the most helpful tools when connecting with a new client.

All colors have different aspects to them. For example, we may see a color that gives a feeling of someone having a strong work ethic and high standards for themselves, yet upon looking deeper, another aspect of this color could be an underlying self-criticism. Imagine being able to feel into the experience that has caused this self-criticism and being able to feel or see where in life this originated. For some people, it can be very validating to be "seen" in this way. Sometimes, another person having an awareness of our experiences without us having to tell them provides immense healing and validation.

Through developing our senses, we may start to become aware of a color system that can be felt or even seen clairvoyantly. You can easily find a definition or dictionary of colors; however, I feel it's much more useful to develop your own color system or definitions, which will allow you to work intuitively.

You can begin doing this by simply noticing how certain colors make you feel. Are there objects in your home that you find comforting? Notice if they have a color palette in common. You might also think of someone in your life, for example, who may be angry, passionate, or action-oriented. Ask yourself, what color do I associate with this person?

EXERCISE: DEVELOPING YOUR COLOR SYSTEM

For this exercise, you will need:

- an empty box or shoebox
- notebook and pen to write
- a blindfold to help you keep your eyes closed

- Several items of varying color that are the same in size. I have used a set of candles in lots of colors, but you could use ribbons or even crayons. Crystals also work well if you have a partner who can add them to the box without you seeing them.
- Blindfold yourself, remove one item from the box and hold it. As you do, notice how it feels in your hand; if you had to assign a temperature to it, would it be hot or cool? What emotion would suit this object—are there any words or images that come to mind? It's important not to force this process but simply allow your intuition to lead you and accept the first thing that comes to mind. If you feel your mind interfering, take a breath to center yourself. This clears the mind for a moment, allowing something else to come through.
- After you've held the object for a moment, open your eyes, write down your impressions, and record the color.
- Discard the current object and choose a new object from the collection box, repeating the process. Record your observations and repeat the process until you move through each color.

14

Kids and Intuition

Kids, like everyone else, are naturally intuitive and sensitive to the world around them. They oftentimes have the benefit of less conditioning preventing them from accessing their intuitive abilities. As our society shifts and becomes more welcoming of these abilities, I believe more and more kids will be open not only to turning towards and talking about their intuition, but also to become practiced in mediumship and psychic work.

As a society, we readily immerse our kids into religion of all kinds but not as commonly to spirituality. This is usually done to protect them—we don't want our kids subject to the consequences of going against social norms. So many of us grew up with almost no real understanding of religious practices or where they stem from, and many of them are outdated, disconnected, or out of line with our actual values.

The more we encourage children to live authentically and embrace sensitivity and awareness, the kinder a society we will create. As a parent, you can create a safe place for your child to explore who they are and help them live in alignment with their own inner knowing. Simple things like encouraging kids to listen to their own hunger cues and eat intuitively or respecting their physical boundaries when they don't want to be hugged or tickled foster, an awareness of and closeness with their intuition.

Helping Kids Get Started

Giving your kids a spiritual foundation can help them lead a more authentic life. As you explore and develop your own intuition, you may feel drawn to share this guide with the children in your life:

You are worthy of love just as you are.

Most parents love their kids unconditionally. As intense as this love is, we may also experience intense fear from the time our kids are born. We have a deep desire to protect and shield them from the world. We sometimes send mixed messages regarding who or what is worthy of our energy. We want them to behave according to society's standards. This is a normal human emotion; the innate human need to "belong to our tribe" is a lifesaving instinct.

When we project our fears onto our kids, we betray the essential message, "You are loved unconditionally." My fear is often triggered each time my kids try something new, interact with other adults that may not respond well to them, or are in a position to make an impression on their peers.

I constantly challenge myself to observe my fear but not act or speak from it. If I can observe the thought "What if your friends judge you for doing that" instead of speaking it, I have an opportunity to learn about myself and truly protect my child from the projection of my own fear.

Be in the moment.

Being present in the moment is perhaps the most valuable life skill we can teach our kids. You may recognize the truth that the present moment is all we have but being conscious of it is not always easy. My son's neuropsychologist once said, "Kids' excessive worrying about the past can lead to depression and kids' excessive worrying about the future can lead to anxiety."

This resonated deeply with me and affirmed my belief that mindfulness is the key to teaching our kids life skills for emotional well-being.

The Spirit World is real.

My kids have always easily accepted this fact. In fact, the same neuropsychologist noted in my son's report that he "heard the voice of his great grandmother who is deceased, but that is not concerning because the family is spiritual and accepts this."

The world is changing—we don't need to protect our kids from closed-minded people at the cost of denying their truth. We all have a voice in our mind, sometimes thoughts running in a constant loop, which—especially for anxious kids—can be quite disturbing.

You are not your thoughts.

As adults, we say things all the time like, "I could just kill them." Thoughts and feelings of anger are natural and if we don't rekindle them, may quickly pass on their own. If kids don't understand that they do not have to identify with these thoughts, that the thoughts are coming from their mind and not their soul or their "true self," it takes a lot of pressure off them.

Our ego often presents itself as our inner monologue constantly criticizing and judging ourselves and others.

Teaching kids that they are more than this inner voice and that they are innately loving at their core allows them to step back from their thoughts instead of identifying with them.

We are all one.

We easily teach "do unto others as you would have done unto you" or in Judaism, "Tikkun Olam," which means "to repair the world." Let's take this one step further with our kids and tell them why.

We are all connected, every living thing originated from the same divine source with a shared purpose for our souls to grow and evolve, and one day return there.

Listen to your body.

Every day, our entire body acts as a psychic antenna for information. Teaching our kids to listen to cues from their bodies when something "doesn't feel right" empowers them to make decisions in their own best interest. Our intuition, subtle energy guidance, or gut instinct is often felt in our solar plexus. Joy and grief are often felt in our heart center. Physical anxiety can be debilitating if we are in a challenging or over-stimulating environment.

Every time we encourage our kids to "push past" fatigue or illness to attend an event or make them "give Grandpa a hug" when they don't want to, we teach them to betray the cues from their own body. Relearning how to listen to our body as an adult is a process many of us struggle with.

Raise your vibration.

In mediumship, we use this expression to explain how we connect with the Spirit World that vibrates at a higher frequency. To act as mediums, we must raise our vibration to meet that of a spirit person.

On the Earth plane, it applies to how loving an individual we are because our vibration can be energetically sensed and felt. When I say "loving," I mean "kind and accepting" not "nice and accommodating." True kindness (speaking kindly of others authentically), setting healthy boundaries, laughter, crying to release emotions, being in nature, and expressing their true selves are all ways for kids to raise their vibration.

Imagine if every human on Earth committed to healing themselves...that would mean peace on Earth. Let us teach that to our kids.

You can't miss out on something that's meant for you.

Too often, we fear that if we "make the wrong decision" we will miss out on something we really want. We all have a divine purpose and what we "think" we want is not always what's best for us. Think of how many missed opportunities were just blessings that led you to something better, something meant for you. While we need to take meaningful action towards our goals and put energy into achieving them, chasing a person or opportunity that is truly meant for us is unnecessary.

Teaching our kids to be more fully themselves will allow the people and opportunities that are meant uniquely for them to naturally come together and be attracted.

This is all temporary.

"This too shall pass" was a favorite saying of my grandmother's and yes heartbreak, loneliness, or despair will all pass. Taking it a step further, acknowledging and understanding that our soul chose to come here for this speck of existence—the idea that we are going to wake up from this life as if waking up from a dream—can be both frightening and freeing at the same time.

If we live our lives as if we are going to experience death like simply waking from a dream, we can face our fears, the greatest of which I believe is to live as we truly are without wearing a mask.

Love isn't painful—attachment is.

Our society idealizes romantic love as all-encompassing, exciting, painful, and dramatic. Let's teach our kids the truth: they do not need another person "to complete them," no one is coming to save them, and they can fill themselves with the love they already have inside of them. Attaching our happiness to another person, place, or job offer is a roadmap to codependency, loneliness, and emptiness. If you have a child, know that they are whole and possess within them everything they need to be fulfilled in this life. It's a privilege and honor to hold space for that. Some of us had parents that taught us these truths through abuse, neglect, or emotional immaturity.

If we have the willingness and ability, we can teach our kids—ultimately teaching them to heal themselves and expand their consciousness—through the message and actions of our own lives.

Kids and Spirit Communication

When parents contact me about their kids communicating with or seeing spirit people, it is often because either they or their kids have had a fearful experience and they are looking for guidance and reassurance. More than anything, sensitive kids need compassion, understanding, and adults who aren't fearful. Young kids are so open to seeing spirit people because they often have no preconceived notions about them. Teaching your kids that the Spirit World is all-loving and will never harm them allows them to develop their own natural and fear-free relationship with the Spirit World.

That said, it is also important to show children how to set boundaries with any spirit communication. Teaching kids to believe that "Please go now" is all that they need to say to the Spirit World, can relieve a lot of anxiety and empower them to set boundaries. Often sensitive kids may become aware of the "energetic footprint" of a place and become aware of people who used to live there.

I commonly (yet unexpectedly) see spirit people in hotel rooms. On one occasion, I was woken up in the middle of the night by a spirit person, a man in a matching pajama set kneeling beside the bed and clutching his chest. I got the sense that he'd had a heart attack in the room many years earlier. This is not the same as connecting with the living energy of a spirit but is often the energetic footprint left behind in a place.

Usually, these images disappear as soon as we decide we don't want them. Clearing your space by burning herbs or using a clearing spray, or with your intention is often all that's needed.

Sometimes, if we are open to it, spirit people can contact us who are a living energy and not only the past energy of a place. When I first started to develop my mediumship abilities, I would often become aware of spirit people at night while I slept. Most often, they would be people I would connect with in my readings the following day. When this happens, I have only to think "Not now, I'm sleeping" and the spirit person vanishes as quickly as they appeared.

Especially for older children, seeing a spirit person may be startling. Teaching kids that they are in control of their abilities will empower them to go at their own pace. If they don't want to see or communicate with a spirit person, kids should know that they may firmly and politely ask them to leave.

The Spirit World has no desire to harm or upset us, but it is still necessary to set boundaries for ourselves.

Kids and Animal Communication

Kids are often brilliant animal communicators. Sensitive kids will sense, know, and sometimes hear what animals are feeling. When my son was five years old, we participated in a therapeutic horseback riding program once a week where he rode a very old, very calm horse named Barney. He always looked forward to lessons and his favorite part was grooming Barney before the lesson.

One time, we went into the stable and greeted Barney, patting him and brushing his sides. The instructor put the saddle on and began to lead him into the ring for our lesson. My son put his helmet on and walked beside Barney, but when it was time to walk into the ring, both Barney and my son refused at the same time. The instructor coaxed Barney along, but my son refused to walk forward saying he could not ride Barney today because "Barney is sick."

The instructor looked concerned and checked the horse over. When she asked my son why he thought Barney was sick, he answered, "His foot hurts."

She looked at each of his feet and said they looked fine. Then she asked my son, "How do you know his foot hurts?"

He answered, "I just know."

The instructor suggested we just give Barney some extra brushing and carrots and said that she would have a vet look at his foot. I was surprised how seriously she took this news of reported illness from a five-year-old. I wondered if she was really going to have a vet come look at him and whispered the question to her as we left. "We have a vet coming by this afternoon anyhow," she said. "It can't hurt."

The following week the instructor greeted us, grinning. "You were right about Barney," she said. "He had an infection in his foot. The vet treated him and he's feeling much better now!"

My son just nodded unimpressed, but I was surprised, so when we got in the car, I asked, "How did you really know he was hurt?"

"He told me." He answered.

EXERCISE: BEGINNING ANIMAL COMMUNICATION

Do you sometimes feel like your family pet is in cahoots with your kids? They most likely are! Kids communicate with animals more easily than adults for several reasons: They are often uninhibited by the idea that they can't communicate—believing you can do something is an important part of success. Kids and animals also benefit from often being at eye level and spending more time in the present moment.

Animal Communication with kids can be fun for everyone involved. If your kids seem interested in communicating with animals, have them "tune in" to the family pet and ask them what they are feeling.

Some questions to tune into or ask your pets are:

- How are they feeling in their body?

- How are they feeling emotionally? Are they feeling bored, stressed, lonely, excited? etc.
- What activities do they most enjoy? Least enjoy?
- What is their favorite place in the house? Why?

Keep this activity as neutral as you would any other casual conversation. This might feel like pretending at first, but you might be surprised at what they report. Keep notes from your conversations so you and your kids can refer to them later.

MORE EXERCISES FOR KIDS

Some of my favorite exercises and intuitive games aren't the ones that are well-thought out and easy to replicate, rather they are the spontaneous ones that develop in fun and natural curiosity. Practicing mentally sending words and thoughts to one another, trying to guess the next number on the dice roll while playing Yahtzee are all ways my kids have practiced receiving information in the moment.

Adopting a relaxed and encouraging attitude as you become more comfortable with your own intuition will also help foster and cultivate it with kids. Remaining neutral or encouraging when someone yells "I heard your thoughts!" or asks the Universe for help with a video game has allowed my kids to develop or not develop their own intuitive abilities without pressure or judgment.

We played this exercise as a game when they were younger—our own version of two truths and a lie:

Explain to your kids that you're going to play a game using their "feeling sense" or intuition. This game is all about feeling or clairsentience. You can have fun with this and use it to get to know one another; chances are, there are lots of things your kids may not know about you.

For each round you will need:

- Pen or pencil
- Three sheets of paper
- Three envelopes

Write down three statements—two that are true and one that is a lie.

For example I might write down:

- I used to sing in a Spice Girl Impersonation group (true)
- I have seen the Aurora Borealis (true)
- I love cauliflower (not true)

Place each statement in a separate envelope and shuffle them. Each statement has the energy of either a truth or a lie, which is one of the easiest feelings for highly sensitive kids to sense. You cannot find these answers with your mind, only through intuition.

Have each player take a deep cleansing breath and hold the statements as they try to feel which one is truth and which is a lie. It is important to encourage a feeling that engages your child's intuition instead of just guessing (which engages the conscious mind).

Remember that since the point of this game is fun and intuitive practice, the emphasis should be on practicing "feeling" and getting to know one another. We all have a conscious mind that is an important part of being human, so we don't need to feel bad when our mind interjects "a guess" instead of our intuition leading us. I like to explain that if we don't get the correct answer, it is not a reflection of our intuitive abilities but rather that some days they are easier than others to access.

Epilogue

Throughout the process of writing this book, I worked hard to stay connected to myself in body, mind, and spirit. The writing process uncovered many painful truths and poked around at old wounds that needed further care. I let myself grieve and process and release pain from my physical body that was still holding on and I have a much deeper understanding of my nervous system and how I am affected by my thoughts and feelings. This process was a gift to myself that has left me feeling freer and truer than I ever thought possible.

There is no end to healing and self-discovery in this life. No final resting space where we get to a point of all-knowing enlightenment and decide to put our feet up and smile in satisfaction knowing that we've ascended beyond painful lessons and illusions. The idea that that place exists is perhaps the greatest illusion.

There are however places we get to visit along the way after we have freed ourselves of false ideas and narratives that feel peaceful, true, and beautiful beyond measure. I find myself now in one of these places as I finish this book. I met my partner Rachel at the beginning of this writing process and the life and home we have built together over the last year is one of these places for me.

Life holds so many surprises and heartbreaks that I await with openness and curiosity. In my work as a medium, I am reminded daily of the grief we all must experience. I am also reminded of the love. The way we are all held by the divine in our darkest moments although we might not feel their presence. We are held just as closely in our joy. Always we are whole, worthy, and enough. In my searching the only place that led me home was inwards towards myself. The amazing healers that I've met on my journey have lovingly directed me back to myself.

This is the direction I hope to have pointed you, dear reader—home to yourself.

ABOUT THE AUTHOR

Sheryl Wagner is a psychic medium and teacher who works with clients from all over the world through private sessions and workshops. Her office is in Canton, Massachusetts, where she lives with her partner Rachel, two teenage sons, and goofy Goldendoodle.

Lightning Source UK Ltd.
Milton Keynes UK
UKHW020644170222
398838UK00008B/361